GW00760133

AHOY THERE

Jack Smith

Acknowledgements

Cover by Alissa Smith
rednutdesign@gmail.com

"Old sailor Jack Smith came to me with a book he was writing about his many years on the seas and the adventures they got up to on the ships – hence the tagline "Contains Salty Language". He wanted a book cover that was a piece of art, so we did some sketches on the spot and came up with the design straight away."

Second edition May 2013
Editing & design: Bev Robitai
www.bevrobitai.co.nz

©*Jack Smith Publishing*
P O Box 32347
Devonport
Auckland NZ 0624

Available on Amazon.com in print or ebook editions.

© Copyright: No part of this publication is to be copied, photocopied or reproduced without written permission of the author.

ISBN 978-0-473-24709-6
New Zealand National Library

For Valerie

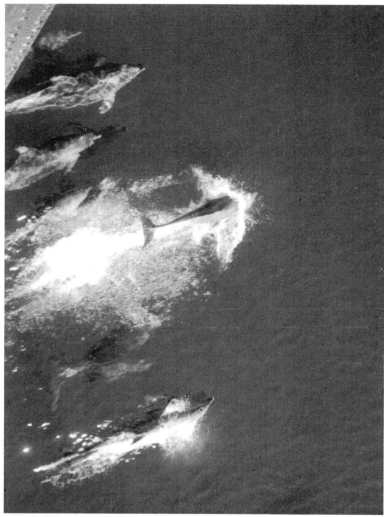

Dolphins at the Bow

Contents

Author's note

Spinning yarns on the poop deck at the end of the day was always something to look forward to. A good raconteur was popular on any ship and there were many good storytellers at sea. Although there were personal tensions at times, humour was a good icebreaker and an important part of life aboard ship.

Most tales were humorous. It was the way a story was told that brought the laughs and often a comic was asked to re-tell a particular story that had done the rounds for years. Stories often started with, "I was on a ship once," or "On my last ship". As one story finished another was started hot on its heels. Even the younger lads got a chance to tell a yarn, but if they tried to tell a story beyond their experience they would be crudely reminded they were still wet behind the ears. "I've wrung more saltwater out of my underpants than you've sailed on, sonny boy."

Women aboard cargo ships were considered bad omens. Occasionally the Captain or Chief Engineer was allowed to take his wife for a trip.

Keeping a sailor's vocabulary in check was a problem at the best of times and females aboard were an unwelcome restriction. The air could be blue when a hammer hit a thumb or a personal item was lost overboard. Seamen were not used to walking around on eggshells.

A favourite joke was when a sailor unknowingly released a loud, healthy fart within earshot of the Captain and his wife taking their afternoon stroll. The red-faced skipper bellowed: "Seaman Smith, how dare you break wind in front of my wife?" To which he replied: "Sorry Captain, I didn't know it was her turn."

Whenever a seaman complained about the food, the lack of overtime, the poor mail service or the absence of a ship's library, invariably his last ship was always better. A constant complainer would be asked bluntly. "If she was that bloody good why did you leave her?" Usually, there would be an excuse such as the bosun was a bastard; I left her in dry dock;

she was a bad feeder; or I got bored with South America. One comic's reason for leaving his last ship was that he'd caught crabs and didn't want to share them with his shipmates.

There were stories about drunken revels, falling in love and jumping ship, jailed around the globe, of fires, mutiny, sabotage, sinkings, sackings and suicides, men running amok with fire axes, others leaping overboard at sea. There were stories of sharks, albatrosses, monkeys, parrots, cats, spiders and cockroaches. There was always a story you hadn't heard before.

Here are just a few.

Jack Smith
Auckland, NZ

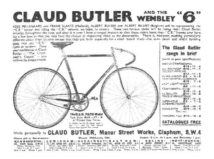

CLAUD BUTLER AND THE WEMBLEY "6"

The Bicycle

The first sign that my name was to be a problem came in 1953 in Brixton, South London.

With two other thirteen-year-old boys from my class at Hackford Road School, I had stolen a bicycle from the school bike shed. The three of us had not pre-planned this escapade – it was very much a spur of the moment decision with probably the only reason being that the first lesson of the day was maths. (Not my favourite subject.)

Brazenly yet furtively we took the bike to a small bike shop in Battersea to sell it. It proved to be a very significant day in my life.

Inexplicably, without nod or consent, I became leader and spokesman. With heart thumping, I strode into the shop. A loud bell clanged above my head as my partners in crime wheeled the bike in behind me.

The friendly dealer was portly with a greasy blue apron and piercing blue eyes. With as much barefaced aplomb as a thirteen-year-old could muster, I said, "Good morning sir, are you interested in buying a bike?" Immediately I knew I should have said 'MY bike' but I knew I could pull this off if I kept a cool head.

Greasy fingers removed the jutting pipe and a puff of smoke rose past the round face.

"How much?"

"Three pounds ten," I said. My throat was dry and I wondered if he could hear my heart thumping.

"You'll have to come back at 2.30. I don't have that kind of money here, OK?" The piercing eyes seemed to glint. "What's your name?"

"John Simpson," I replied calmly.

"And you two?"

From behind me came "George Fowler" then "Peter O'Donnell." To my relief they'd given false names too and had sounded calm. I felt excited and confident.

"Can you come back at 2.30, lads?"

"Yes," I said firmly. Those smiling eyes seemed to be drilling holes through to my very soul.

We eased ourselves out of the oily, claustrophobic shop onto busy Battersea Road. The chill air felt icy on my face – I was sweating and hoped the dealer hadn't noticed.

We whiled away the time in a transport café drinking strong tea until it was time to return to the shop, congratulating ourselves on a job well done and speculating how we would spend the money – cigarettes and cream cakes were high on the list.

The time arrived to return to the shop. We reassured each other on the way with reminders to stay calm and leave the talking to me.

Strangely, the bell above the door seemed to ring louder and longer as we filed in expectantly. The dealer immediately appeared from the back room again but this time another man followed. Something was wrong here. We were just wrestling with understanding this new situation when the door behind us opened and the bell sounded like a klaxon. I spun around to see a tall man in an overcoat and trilby hat, framed between the swivelled heads of my partners in crime.

The scarred face was not friendly. A heavy moustache below a broken nose was turning grey, and the eyes were cold button black.

"Good afternoon, boys. My name is Detective Charles Parker." The voice was flat, Scottish and matter-of-fact.

My whole body suddenly felt cold and I had an instant desire to urinate. Both my companions turned and looked at me with an accusing panic in their eyes. This was not lost on Detective Parker.

The dealer brought the bike out from the back room like a prized possession. It looked larger now, and was certainly worth a lot more than three pounds ten shillings. It was a Claud Butler racing bike (the Rolls Royce of cycles at that time) and had the initials FM carved deeply into the racing saddle. Big mistake – none of our names either false or genuine matched the initials.

Detective Parker was in full control. All the exits were blocked. There was nowhere to run.

"Before we begin, I want you all to know I can't abide liars." A notebook magically flicked open in his hand, a pencil touched his tongue, but the black eyes never moved. The stabbing pencil aimed at me.

"You, what's your name?"

"John Smith," I replied.

A white flash blinded me – there was an explosion in my left ear and I landed on the greasy floor between my cohorts' shaking legs, holding my rapidly-swelling cheek.

The rest of the interrogation was very brief.

It was my first brush with the law.

The box-like Black Maria never once rang its silver bell as it carted us to Brixton Police station. I felt both cheated and dejected. Detective Parker followed smugly in a polished police car.

We were put in separate cells while they summoned our parents. This was not an easy task for none of our families boasted a telephone. It took some hours.

Meanwhile, an evening meal of sausages, eggs and baked beans with a thick slice of buttered bread was delivered to my cell. I wolfed it down thinking they might have mistaken me for another prisoner. Briefly I felt very special. Certainly it was the most memorable meal of my life at that time.

Eventually a silent prison guard with a beckoning finger took me along a whitewashed corridor, his steel-heeled boots and jangling keys making a musical sound as I kept pace with him.

Opening a heavy wooden door, he propelled me into a room then was gone.

The Chief Inspector sat behind a long wooden table with a sheaf of paper, his silvered cap, and a stern look. The other two boys stood at the table with heads bowed, with their fathers behind them. They had been waiting for my mother, who stood against the granite wall with arms folded and fumed. I took the indicated spot at the table alone.

The inspector sighed loudly. "I want you all to have these boys at Brixton Magistrates' Court next Monday morning at 10am."

Mr Gleeson clamped a hand on his son's shoulder. "He'll be there, Inspector."

Mr Thomas clipped his son's ear and said the same.

The inspector swung towards my mother. "And you, madam?"

"But he might run away, Inspector." There was despair in her voice.

"Then we'll make sure he doesn't."

That night I was sent to a remand home in North London. The other boys went home with their dads.

The Juvenile Court was crowded and finally I faced the judge – a black-robed old vulture who stared down at me.

"Why was this boy detained and the others not?" he asked.

"His mother said he might run away m'Lord," said a voice.

The shoulders went up as the head came down. Two watery eyes appeared over thick glasses resting on the beaked nose.

"John Smith," he chuckled. "It says here he wants to go to sea."

"Yes m'Lord," the voice said.

The other two received nine months' probation. I spent two years and three months in an approved nautical school on

4

the windswept Northumberland coast. Blyth was a long way from Brixton.

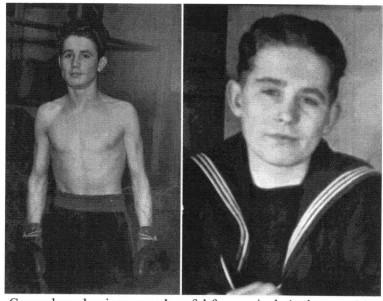

Compulsory boxing proved useful for survival. Author age 14.

The Dartwood (my first ship)

My First Hamburger

On my first trip to sea in 1956 we sailed from South Africa and headed to the port of Baltimore, Maryland. The Chesapeake Bay was cold and crisp in early winter and contained more warships than I'd ever seen in one place.

The American Atlantic fleet had returned from manoeuvres and the whole bay was full of warships of every shape and size in what seemed an endless convoy, stretching to the distant grey horizon.

From Baltimore we went to Norfolk, Virginia, a US Navy's Home Port, to load military equipment for, as yet, an unnamed port in Central America. Gangs of well-dressed longshoremen wearing hard hats clambered up the gangway with aluminium lunchboxes and thermos flasks under a cloud of cigar smoke with drawls heard only in cowboy movies. Some of them were Negroes. They took over the ship in the most deliberate and efficient manner and were most particular with safety before anything else. They were very different to the singing, ragged workers in South Africa. I was in a different world.

"Hey you, Limey kid, where's the john?" The cigar was pointing at me.

"Which John would you like?" I replied. I was saved from further embarrassment when one of the crew pointed to the toilet.

"Don't react to being called a Limey. They're Yanks, we're Limeys. Get used to it."

The galley-boy and I went ashore to check out the town while the rest of the crew happily housed themselves in the nearest bar.

Unlike in Britain, we were minors in the USA and the laws were strict; sixteen-year-olds were not served alcohol.

There were plenty of sights for two young Limey lads to feast their eyes on, so we wandered around, unashamedly gawking at people wearing cowboy hats, hand-tooled boots and ornate belt buckles.

Guns were everywhere; trucks had racks of shotguns in their cabs and in the Sheriff's patrol car, a sad looking bloodhound eyed our passing. It was a surreal sight to this boy from Brixton, London, England.

We arrived at a crossroad with a huge American flag floating above an equally huge neon sign stating DRUGS and FOOD. Big brightly coloured cars laden with chromium were casually parked, unlocked with the windows open. It was an impressive sight.

We wandered into a shopping mall that housed clothing, liquor, hardware, drug, gun and food stores. Here we were stared at in return for we were the only ones not wearing a uniform.

We followed our noses to a wonderful smell of hotdogs and hamburgers and found two chrome barstools at a horseshoe-shaped red Formica bar trimmed with yet more chrome. On my left was a large laughing Negro torpedo-man festooned with service badges, with a toothy girlfriend dressed in pink.

Politely we waited and watched a leathery-faced matron, shrouded in steam, frying steaks, bacon and eggs, hot dogs, onions, hamburgers and French fries. With a utensil in each

7

hand, she flipped and turned the sizzling food while taking very complicated orders from the circle of diners.

"Hey lady, gimme a double-decker cheese with large fries and Cola will yer?"

"I'll have three hot dogs with fries and coffee, easy on the onions. OK?"

"Gimme bacon, eggs sunny side up, hash browns and black coffee."

I'd heard that the Americans were very polite but I listened in sheer disbelief to these young Yanks throwing food orders at the sweating matron without a single please or thank-you.

Suddenly, the impatient matron was pointing one of her utensils at me from under a veil of steam. "YOU, WADDERYERWANT?" she demanded. I was abruptly brought out of my reverie, red-faced, and blurted out: "Two hamburgers, if you don't mind, please."

"Why the hell should I mind, it's my job, ain't it?" she spat back. She then mumbled something over her shoulder that I couldn't understand.

"I beg your pardon, could you repeat that please?" Hissing, she spun to face me with clenched fists on hips. "I said, do you want goddam coleslaw?"

My terribly British accent and over-the-top politeness was not cutting any ice with this fierce matron, who was riding a storm.

By now we had attracted the attention of the other diners; we were obviously aliens in their territory. The torpedo-man asked where we hailed from; then called across the bar to his buddy: "Hey Elmer, come over here and listen to these Limeys talking, will yer?" As I shook his hand, I said to Elmer: "Terribly charmed to meet you, old chap." Even the matron joined the eruption of laughter.

Our burgers, fries and Cola were paid for with much backslapping, while on the jukebox, Hank Williams sang, 'Your Cheating Heart'.

Full of food and smoking cigars, we headed back to the ship reflecting on how very kind the Americans were.

Reaveley

Chicken

The British Merchant Navy was not known for its culinary excellence and tramp ships had the worst reputations when it came to feeding their crews.

In the port of Sunderland the *Reaveley* was preparing for sea and signing-on a crew for parts unknown.

Tramps held the promise of excitement; visiting every corner of the globe and never knowing your destination until you actually arrived there.

On a voyage to Africa, the cargo could be sold to someone in Japan or India while still on the high seas and consequently a "Change of Orders" brought about an "Altering of Course". Cheers for Osaka, boos for Bombay. With their reputation for bad food and trips of up to two years away from home, experienced seamen avoided the shipping office until tramps like the *Reaveley* had left port.

Looking for adventure and wanting to see more of the world, I signed on as a junior ordinary seaman, not caring how long the voyage, or how bad the food.

On the first Sunday at sea there was a buzz of excitement among the crew because chicken was on the menu. Chicken was a rarity on a British tramp ship.

9

Geordie, the self-appointed leader of the crew, was a large able seaman in his early thirties whose upper torso had been fully tattooed over many years, in his travels around the globe. His braying Tyneside accent was always at its thickest when he was angry or excited and today he was excited about the chicken.

It was noon in the deck-hands' mess room, and big Geordie had something to say and when Geordie had something to say, he expected people to listen, and we did.

One meaty tattooed hand gripped a small mallet, while the hula girl under the palm tree on his forearm wriggled as he shifted his grip. He had our undivided attention.

"Peggy, gan an get wor soom neels from the chippy."

The deck-boy was gone in a flash.

"Now, I'll tell yers what we're ganna dee lads. We'll knock a line of neels reet aroon the mess room bulkheads, and every time we have chicken we'll hang a wishbone on one of the neels." Geordie looked smug.

Another able seaman, not yet accepting Geordie's top-dog status, questioned him loudly. "Why, what the hell would you want to do that for, Geordie?"

Geordie stuck out his chin and lifted his ample stomach to his chest and snorted. "Are yee stupid or something? Why, when we get back hoom at the end of the trip, we'll knae how many times we had chicken. Haven't yee got any brains lad?"

That was the last time Geordie was challenged by the now red-faced challenger.

The deck-boy returned with a bag of nails; Geordie hammered them high on the bulkhead in a neat line and with a satisfied grin, announced that we could also use them to hang up our oilskins.

We tramped around for nearly a year; to Canada, America, Panama, Mexico, Japan, Ocean Island, Australia and India, enduring the awful ship's food with weevils and cockroaches.

There were many memorable events on the long voyage and Geordie made sure we were all tattooed in Bombay.

Chicken never appeared again. At least not in the crew's mess room. At the end of the voyage and nearly a whole year later there was still only one wishbone on the line of rusty nails.

Reaveley crew, Panama 1957

Author 4th from L, smoking – the James Dean look.

Esso London (T2 tanker)

The Shortest Trip

I transferred from South Shields Shipping Pool to the Dock St Pool in the heart of London's East End and booked into the Flying Angel Seamen's home.

I loved the narrow cobbled streets of Aldgate; the many shops with cheerful Jewish traders bantering loudly. The barbershops placed steaming towels on a freshly shaved chin and jokes galore were served with a splash of Bay Rum. The local London rhyming slang flew across my favourite café as I observed the world through dank lace curtains.

I was very happy to be back home in London after years away.

I bought my first pair of blue suede shoes and bounced into the shipping office ready to take on the world. A blackboard listed ship's names in need of crews; so many ABs for this one, three stewards for another, plus a fireman for yet another. An old timer with a horridly scarred face explained them all. He was a survivor from a torpedoed tanker during the war.

I took an Ordinary Seaman's job on the oil tanker *Esso London* and the following day I was sent to Southampton by train. She was an American-built wartime T2 Tanker, basic with no frills. She was on a regular shuttle service taking oil from the refinery at Saltend near Hull to Southampton.

Lugging my suitcase up the steep gangway in the dark, I stepped into an unfamiliar setting. Everything was different and strange.

There were no hatches, no derricks and no rigging, just huge pipes and valves everywhere. The only ropes were mooring ropes.

I found the grumpy bosun asleep on his bunk, boots and all. He took my details then led me to an empty 4-berth cabin. "You're on the 12–4 watch, we sail at 0200." He disappeared with a grunt. A feminine, balding steward with bad teeth supplied me with linen and watched as I made up the only empty bunk. "Anything you want, young man, come to your Uncle George. I was once Queen Bee with Cunard." He told me that my predecessor, a very nice boy called Jimmy, had accidentally jammed his penis in his rusty personal effects drawer and was now in Southampton Hospital in the hands of the nurses. After a shower, he'd had a habit of shutting the drawer with his muscular thighs once too often. "Now you be careful young man." He minced off.

My cabin mates arrived back aboard – not one was sober.

Once out in the Channel, I was left alone as the lookout and I huddled against the freezing night reporting ships' lights by ringing the bell. I wasn't there long before Taffy, an AB., took over asking me to relieve the helmsman in his place because he was too drunk.

It would be a great favour to be returned; no one would notice in the dark and it would be warmer on the wheel.

Inside the wheelhouse it was jet black except for the green glow from the compass that showed the craggy face of the wheelman who gave me the ship's course then promptly vanished.

The second mate worked alone on charts behind a curtain under a dimmed light. Soon we were in the busy English Channel and I struggled to keep her on course. The ship started to swing off course then, suddenly, somewhere in the darkness, a loud, rapid clicking sound was heard followed by a banshee scream of panic.

The second mate threw me roughly aside, grabbed the wheel and brought her back on course, showering me with enough curses to last me a lifetime.

In the morning I found myself in front of a furious captain with a grim-looking bosun alongside. My services were no longer required. On our return to Southampton I would be discharged, then sent back to London.

"Imagine the catastrophe you could have created. Tankers are no place for cowboys like you. I suggest you go back to cargo ships for all our sakes."

Taffy avoided me. I was a sacrificial lamb.

There was a special moment on returning to Southampton when we passed close to the liner *Queen Mary* leaving for New York. Dwarfed by the magnificent, massive vessel, I wondered what might have been when I was zigzagging a few nights before.

Six days after signing on I was back on the train for an uneventful journey back to London, hoping that Taffy would jam *his* prick in that rusty drawer.

Baltic Express

Frigid Finland

The Shipping Master was sympathetic to my plight and signed me on a brand new ship, still in the builder's yard in Hamburg.

On the morning of 25 November 1957, crews with their bags packed the shipping office with excited chatter, joining ships going around the globe. Our crew for the *Baltic Express* filed into a train that took us to Harwich for the ferry across the North Sea to the Hook of Holland en route to Hamburg.

The ferry rolled like a pig, which had some travellers helplessly emptying their stomachs in a chain reaction. The stench was awful in the closed spaces. I joined the crew in the bar for the overnight trip and made a mental note never to take a job on a ferry.

Another bus took us through the Hamburg streets showing both the ruin and rebuilding. The bus was strangely subdued as the crew contemplated the animus of the recent war. I felt a strange mix of awe and admiration for these people who had bombed us into underground shelters, not so long ago.

The floodlit ship was a sight to behold. Painted white, with sleek, racy lines and sparkling new under a light coating of snow, she was more like a yacht than any ship I had seen. Stores were loaded while welders spat and sparked with last minute adjustments as we hauled our bags aboard. Down below, the smell of new paint and varnish was a refreshing change from the old tanker I'd left behind.

My compact 2-berth cabin was perfect luxury with matching curtains on bunks and porthole, plus a chest of drawers with a bookshelf above. Blankets, towels, sheets and pillow were all brand new with no previous stains. I knew I would be very happy aboard the *Baltic Express*.

Unable to sleep, I chatted with the local night watchman till the wee small hours. He was glad to have someone to talk to. He was in his late seventies and I was just seventeen. He had been a young gunner aboard the German Cruiser *Emden* in the first World War and he'd survived its sinking. The crew was allowed to use the name Emden as a hyphenated addition to their names in recognition for their heroic actions. I liked that touch.

We sailed from the yard with an exciting fanfare from tooting tugs and cheering workers on other vessels nearing completion; someone had a bugle.

We were headed through the Kiel Canal into the Baltic Sea heading for Finland. On a cold and bleak afternoon we berthed in the port of Kotka for our very first cargo. Men and women in fur-lined quilted clothes loaded us with large logs, processed timber, sheets of plywood and cartons of matches by the thousands.

Invited to a dance that night, we donned our best English suits and crunched through the hardened snow to the local wooden community hall for some fun. The whole interior was lined with bare plywood sheets and on a wooden stage a band of young lads flailed their wooden guitars and wailed at the wooden ceiling. 'Blueberry Hill' sounded hilarious in Finnish. Chilled, low-alcohol beer ensured there was always a queue for the single wooden toilet and in that queue, I met Pepsi and instantly fell in love.

16

We waltzed to Pepsi's favourite song, 'Island in the Sun' then I walked her home while a boy with acne discreetly followed. We kissed in doorways; her curly blonde hair trimmed the hood that framed her bright blue eyes and rosy cheeks. She was everything the pop songs sang about.

Her maddening perfume had me enlivened with ardent need and I fumbled with her many layers as my toes froze in my damp blue suede shoes. Giggling patiently, Pepsi removed my icy fingers from their groping journey until she answered her mother's call. Full pink lips met mine with whispered hurried arrangements to meet at the hall for a movie the next night.

I was in heaven.

But hell was the agony returning to the ship, doubled over with pain and needing feverish relief behind a snow-caked wooden fence. Relating my story to an older shipmate in the morning brought hearty laughter. "You had a bad case of lover's bollocks, son." That evening Pepsi and I were glued together, watching an American Western with the acne youth watching furtively nearby. Dark-headed boys like me were popular with the Baltic and Nordic girls while the reverse was true for blond boys in South America.

I was crestfallen leaving Kotka because Pepsi's father refused to allow her to wave me goodbye.

Topping up the cargo in the port of Turku I was indifferent to anything but Kotka and Pepsi; I was also the butt of jokes among the crew. Across the Baltic, through the Kattegat and Skagerrak to the port of Hull I thought only of Pepsi. I sent her Harry Belafonte singing her favourite song, a photograph and our return date with oceans of love and waves of kisses.

Flying back across the North Sea the *Baltic Express* seemed to quiver on every wave. Sixteen knots was fast but not fast enough for me.

Back through the Skagerrak and Kattegat, back into the Baltic happily heading for Finland and Pepsi at good speed when freezing fog slowed us down.

Double lookouts were posted. The foghorn reverberated forlornly through the thick white blanket as the fo'c'sle bell clanged non-stop into the eerie gelid air. We were isolated from the rest of the world for many extra hours.

Then magically the fog lifted to reveal a sight I would never forget. There on the ice floe were two fur-wrapped men pulling a light boat behind them. One was the pilot to take us to Kotka. We came gently alongside the ice, the pilot climbed our ladder and we were on our way again. Leaving the assistant on the ice with his boat we followed a Russian icebreaker into the port of Kotka where bad news awaited me.

The pallid lad with the acne gleefully informed me through bad breath that Pepsi's father had taken a diplomatic post in New York and moved the whole family to America. My heart sank.

Again we loaded the same cargo in the same ports but now Finland was a grim, joyless place without Pepsi. The return voyage began with the Russian icebreaker tearing up the ice for our way to open sea, the last vessel out before the Baltic Sea froze and closed for the winter.

On the first night we ran into a fierce storm with sea spray freezing instantly to our masts, railings and rigging. Each crashing wave built a huge, dangerous, top-heavy, block of ice above deck. The ship was slowed to half-speed with every man aboard working like a beaver under floodlights, smashing at the ice with hammers, crowbars and shovels to rid us of the unwanted extra weight.

Eventually the storm abated. Daylight brought relief and a satisfied grin to every face. We had saved the ship from certain disaster. The London-bound cargo found us heading up the Thames on a 3am tide still with Baltic ice on our masts and rigging with the hatches frozen solid.

Another voyage was at an end. I'd seen enough ice for now. So it was back to the tropics for me.

'Island in the Sun' was my favourite ballad in the rocking year of 1958 thanks to beautiful, blonde, blue-eyed Pepsi from frigid Finland.

The photo I sent Pepsi. Author age 17.

MV. St Thomas

South America

Valerie's father was a detective in the Metropolitan Police who offered me a warm room with his family in a police flat in south-east London while I prepared for my next step up the nautical ladder.

Dusty would take me around his patch introducing me to spivs and barrow-boys who carried out their business in the pubs around the Old Kent Road.

When Dusty walked into a pub, the hush indicated that a copper had arrived and a glass of ale was quickly supplied by a fawning larrikin who had fallen foul of Dusty, or was about to.

With a penetrating eye that missed nothing, Dusty was not above dealing out old-fashioned justice in the lanes and alleys behind the pubs. A broken nose was testament to his prowess in the police boxing squad in his heyday.

Achieving my Lifeboat and Efficient Deck Hands Certificate brought me a major pay rise. Now at eighteen years, no longer a Boy Rating, I was growing up fast.

I signed on the *Saint Thomas* belonging to the South American Saint Line as an EDH in February 1958. We loaded general cargo in London, Rotterdam, Antwerp and Hamburg with many new Volkswagen cars secured below decks. I sat in one, admiring the excellent workmanship and loving the smell of a brand new car.

Chinese cooks provided excellent food and I had my very first single cabin next to the Chinese quarters. My initial complaint about the late night noise of slapping Mah Jong tiles fell on deaf ears. I was advised not to upset them; they were very good cooks with very large knives.

A few of the crew had short-wave radios, so we were always able to keep in touch with world news and the football results. It was a happy crew with no fights; the result of good food, good accommodation, good weather and good ports ahead.

After many scorching days and balmy starlit nights, our first landfall was the port of Recife in northern Brazil. It was hot and humid. The main street from the port was classic Wild West frontier stuff, straight from the movies.

The people, a rich mix of races, predominantly Negro with absolutely no racial intolerance, made a refreshing change from South Africa. Here the police chief was a Negro with many medals.

Lively Latin music burst from every bar, while the smell of cooking beef floated on the air.

One night in a bar we witnessed a dispute between a local couple. They yelled and slapped each other until he grabbed her arm and swung her in a wide circle, scattering tables, drinkers and glasses as one. He stood with a glazed look in his eyes and a knife in his hand. No one moved. It seemed everything was in slow motion until the woman let out a long loud scream. A short stout policeman strutted through the batwing doors with his gun drawn. He fired a shot into the ceiling, took the knife from the distraught drunk then strutted out again leaving him behind. That was the end of the matter and normal services were quickly resumed.

Early morning arrival in Rio de Janeiro was a stunning sight in an already warm day. The clouds lifted to reveal the famous Statue of Christ high above the city as we cruised to our berth in the crowded port.

Exotic musty smells blended with perfume and coffee was a heady mix after weeks at sea and fuelled my expectations of this famous port. Pink and lilac-coloured colonial buildings and apartments seemed unreal as we eagerly hurried ashore through the noise of tooting traffic.

The famous Florida Bar was our destination. As renowned as New York's Market Diner, Quinn's Bar in Tahiti, Ma Gleeson's in Auckland and the Roundhouse in London, it was high on the list of favourite seamen's bars. It was huge, noisy and opened to the street with seamen from around the globe crowded around the tables, enjoying time ashore.

Hustlers, hawkers and shoeshine boys expertly worked among the free-spending sailors while a brass band blasted out the Latin beat. Laughing, dusky girls worked the age-old trade, coming and going with customers at will. Our table was reduced to three from the original eight at times; the lads returning with satisfied smiles.

I resisted many offers of a "short time" until a late hour when a stunning, dark-skinned girl stood in front of me and took my hand. She led me unashamedly through the tables into the hot night. Quickly we were accosted by an angry Military Policeman carrying a large automatic and a belligerent scowl under his helmet. Heated words flashed between them.

My rum and bravado was quickly dampened when I looked into his murderous eyes before she led me firmly away. In the safety of a hotel room she explained that they were once lovers.

The dawn came too soon. Her embrace and our final clasping shower completed an unforgettable first experience in Rio, a world away from Pepsi in Finland. I never knew her name, nor she mine. I never saw her again but I took her lingering sweet smell back to the ship for a few more hours of pleasure.

Sailing into Buenos Aires we passed the scuttled hulk of the famous *Admiral Graf Spee*, the German warship scuttled by her Captain Lansdorf, when trapped by the British Cruisers *Achilles, Ajax* and *Exeter* in the Battle of the River Plate.

We discharged the last of our cargo in Buenos Aires then moved up river to Rosario to load frozen beef for England. Huge chains embedded in the bank moored us to a wooden wharf in the flowing river. Attached to the wharf was an abattoir and freezing works surrounded by herds of cattle being funnelled into pens by lively, yelling gauchos.

There was no nightlife here but there was fun and excitement. The locals hired us their horses for a few pesos and laughed at our inept attempts at riding. One of the crew was badly lacerated along a barbed wire fence by his unresponsive mount. He needed stitches to an arm and a leg.

I had studied cowboys in the movies so my first time on a horse was to be thrilling and without fear.

The feisty ball of quivering muscle took off in a rush with me hanging onto its mane, my feet in rope stirrups, and minus a saddle. I finished my first session in a muddy lake, ejected by a snorting horse with a flicking tail and bulging eyes.

Back in the port of Buenos Aires to complete loading I discovered a laughing girl named Loretta in the Lighthouse Bar and was again smitten.

Beautiful, laughing Loretta, with a handful of others, milked the customers for exorbitantly priced drinks, which were listed as their earnings behind the bar. It was just cola. Loretta milked me for plenty till the early hours then left me with a laughing kiss to meet an American sailor for a pre-arranged booking.

At her request I hastened back the following night. She squealed with delight on my arrival and I sat smugly watching her weaving her web on others, knowing that tonight was my night. Strict curfews were still in place from the Peronista years, so bar girls left unescorted to avoid arrest.

As dawn broke I was taken by taxi to a suburban street, then left to await Loretta. For a while I thought that I had been the butt of a cruel joke until the taxi returned and Loretta swept me into a hotel foyer. Her apartment had the biggest bed I'd ever seen, plus a well-stocked bar with a uniformed, middle-aged maid to bring food at the press of a button.

For a long magical weekend, Loretta bathed, massaged and pampered me.

Lying on her silky bed, she showed me an album of photographs of young lads from around the globe. She knew all their names. When she added mine I knew that I would return to Buenos Aires.

We loaded a team of polo ponies for the British Royal Family collection into wooden stables on the after deck with a gaucho in charge. As he spoke no English, he preferred to sleep with his ponies at night time and worked with them nonstop during the daytime, adjusting their belly straps and tethers.

On Sundays he would don his traditional black outfit – a black hat with silver coins in the band, a silver buckled belt and silver spurs on his black shiny boots. His lively, dark button eyes and constant smile brought a happy difference to the homeward voyage. I regularly tested my Spanish with him.

Laughing Loretta in the Lighthouse and South America had left an indelible mark on me.

RMS Highland Monarch

The Highland Monarch

Royal Mail Lines ran regular passenger/cargo ships between Britain and South America. They had the biggest fleet on that run. London was the home port; the head office was in the city of London. General cargo was shipped outward bound then, frozen Argentine beef was shipped homeward bound.

I joined the *Highland Monarch* in King George V dock in September 1958 and a week later we sailed down the Thames to Tilbury where the passengers embarked. Gold braid and uniforms were everywhere. From the captain and mates, the pursers, the chief engineer and his many underlings, the chief steward with his vast staff to the master-at-arms and his two assistants, they all sported gold braid.

The bosun wore a peaked cap, brass buttons on his coat and crossed anchors on his sleeve. Scores of perfumed stewards had epaulettes on their starched white jackets. Aboard the *Highland Monarch* things were regimented and orderly. It was my first passenger ship and it had two funnels.

First-class passengers promenaded around the upper decks with an air of satisfaction while third-class passengers were crammed into lower decks close to the engine room. Our quarters, wedged into the bows of the ship, were a rabbit warren, well away from the passengers.

I shared an airless cabin with five deck-hands and many cockroaches. A tin of sweetened condensed milk was issued to each deck-hand every ten days for use in tea. The cockroaches loved the stuff. Basic food was cooked in a crew galley, a world apart from the fine foods served on the upper decks.

We loaded Spanish peasants with mountains of baggage in the port of Vigo, then another batch of Portuguese peasants in Lisbon seeking a new life in Brazil and Argentina.

Early morning holystoning (scrubbing) the teak decks was a physical and enjoyable start to each day. An orderly line of sailors with large blocks of pumice attached to long wooden shafts swung them in unison under the watchful eye of the bosun's mate.

One hot day crossing the Atlantic, a frail old man travelling with a private nurse died. Rumour said that he was an ex-Navy Admiral with no luggage, that he had taken this voyage to be buried at sea. I remembered observing him being assisted aboard at Tilbury dressed in pajamas, gown and slippers.

With another deck-hand, I was selected to assist the lamp trimmer on an upper deck to sew the body into a crude canvas bag while the passengers were below enjoying their midday meal. On our knees and dripping sweat, we fitted iron bars into the base of the bag while the chief mate, doctor and nurse looked on. The ship slowed. A Red Ensign was draped over the body. A bible appeared. A prayer was read. We raised the end of the hatch board and watched the wrapped body drop into the sea with a splash. Afloat for a while, it slowly disappeared into Neptune's arms watched by our sombre group of six.

The canvas and twine were gathered. The flag was furled. The ship resumed its speed. We were given a tot of rum, then sent back to work at the end of a man's life. Meanwhile, below in the dining saloon, crystal glasses and silver spoons tinkled, unknowingly.

Then, on another hot day I discovered sores on my scrotum. Perhaps it was the crowded conditions or a tropical bug, whatever it was my cabin mates couldn't agree when I first displayed my sack. But they all agreed I should see the quack. Quick.

The doctor held a short crew session each day prior to his three-course lunch with the jewelled ladies and whiskered gents at the Captain's table. The short balding nurse had me prepared naked on a table with a rubber sheet when the doctor arrived in his starched white, gold-braided tropical uniform. He removed the thermometer from my mouth, checked the reading with a flick then used it to move my testicles around with a look of disdain. I could smell gin on his breath as he solemnly mixed a pink paste onto a wad of white lint and applied it to my scrotum. With my back arched and legs apart a bandage was passed around my groin, under my back, then across my stomach many times.

The nurse developed a dry cough, gently patting the pad with each passing until my scrotum was fully encased. I struggled to avoid any thoughts that would enhance my now creeping virility and fought desperately to stay limp while they muttered about the difficulty of dressing such a part of the anatomy. Large scissors appeared in the nervous nurse's hand. He snipped the bandage at my navel just as my maleness sprang from its place of rest on my left thigh.

I shut my eyes waiting for the pain, but miraculously, a small nip on the tip and a minute blob of blood was the only damage to my swiftly softening sailor's salute. The doctor counselled control as he departed for his lunch. The nurse, now minus his cough, handed me fresh lint and bottle of iodine with a facetious smile. Around the captain's table the ladies laughed lustily.

Arrival in Rio was glorious pandemonium with thousands of people waving and cheering from both ship and jetty. Once berthed, the passengers from Portugal streamed down the gangways into the waiting arms of long-lost loved ones, oblivious to the booming voice of the master-at-arms announcing the well-worn public address call.

"All ashore that's going ashore."

One pioneering first-class passenger had his open-top Rolls Royce gingerly lowered among a pile of cabin trunks to take the drive to Buenos Aires with his lady wife. Finally the hubbub abated then the crew were allowed ashore. With a scented letter from Loretta in my back pocket I avoided the clamour of the Florida Bar, satisfied with a cable-car trip to the famous statue of Christ looking down on the miniature liners far below.

"All visitors ashore" was a welcomed call as the *Highland Monarch* prepared to sail south for Buenos Aires and Loretta.

Sitting on a barstool facing the door, she let out her practised squeal of delight, planted her lovely lips on mine and requested a drink. She was as beautiful as ever and I was ecstatic being with her again. Later that evening she left me to comfort a handsome, Swedish lad sitting alone in a booth. Blond hair was much preferred by the dark-haired Latin girls. She came back explaining that my blond competition was sailing for home in the morning. "You understand, Johnny." Yes, I understood.

I enjoyed the following evenings in the plush apartment where we talked and laughed and I came to terms with her profession. I sailed back to Loretta many times, happy to be one of her favourites with my photo in her album.

By now the *Highland Monarch* and her sister ships were nearing the end of their service and were ready for the scrap yard. She had been my home for a year and was to be replaced by a new class of liner.

Although I would miss laughing Loretta, it was time to sail new seas.

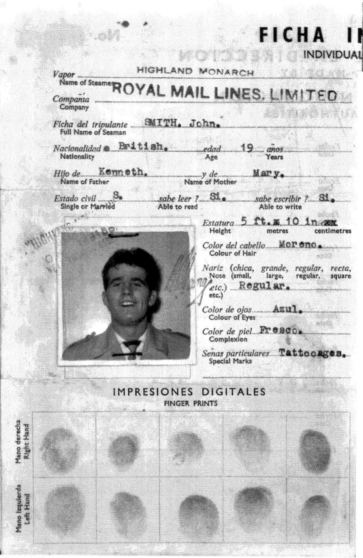

FICHA I

INDIVIDUAL

Vapor
Name of Steamer HIGHLAND MONARCH

Compañia ROYAL MAIL LINES, LIMITED
Company

Ficha del tripulante SMITH. John.
Full Name of Seaman

Nacionalidad British. *edad* 19 *años*
Nationality   Age   Years

Hijo de Kenneth. *y de* Mary.
Name of Father   Name of Mother

Estado civil S. *sabe leer ?* Si. *sabe escribir ?* Si.
Single or Married   Able to read   Able to write

Estatura 5 ft. x 10 in. cm.
Height   metres   centimetres

Color del cabello Moreno.
Colour of Hair

Nariz (chica, grande, regular, recta,
Nose (small, large, regular, square
etc.) Regular.
etc.)

Color de ojos Azul.
Colour of Eyes

Color de piel Fresco.
Complexion

Señas particulares Tattooages.
Special Marks

IMPRESIONES DIGITALES
FINGER PRINTS

Mano derecha / Right Hand

Mano izquierda / Left Hand

Argentine paper passport

29

English Star

Royal Star

Blue Star

The Blue Star Line had ships that went everywhere and their funnels were the most outstanding among all others anywhere on the globe. Everywhere you went there would be a Blue Star ship in port.

I joined the MV *English Star* in London's Victoria Docks in August 1959 for a home trade run running between British and European ports while the permanent crew enjoyed their leave.

Blue Star Line also preferred fit, hardworking and well-behaved seamen aboard their ships, so this was to be my opportunity to show my worth to a new company. While in London Docks, all the bathrooms and toilets were locked and all hands used toilets ashore. Both the British and Asiatic-type toilets were available and both were to be avoided if possible. They were not very clean.

One morning after a night on the town, I had an urgent pressure to make a quick visit to the nearest one. A shallow, sloping trough ran along one wall with small divisions that offered minimal privacy. You could read the next man's newspaper and see a line of straining faces if you wished. It was very Victorian.

Those at the lower end of the trough endured the higher one's evacuations floating past below them. A wooden strip on the edge of the trough was your seat while scraps of damp newspaper were the only cleaning aids.

The next day I was furiously scratching my groin. I had caught a dose of 'Sandy McNabs' CRABS. Shaving off my pubic hair was followed by a frantic lunchtime visit to the nearest chemist shop; my only chance just prior to sailing.

The attractive young assistant was eager to help while I was scratching my itch below the counter out of sight. I asked if she had anything for lice. She happily presented me with a bottle of blue lotion with a guarantee of giving my hair lots of bounce.

I patiently explained lice on the body but not on the head. With her back turned I had another furious scratch.

Yes, she understood and returned with another proffered bottle which was to rid me of dandruff too.

My ship was sailing, my balls were itching and I was getting nowhere fast. "Is there a man here?" I blurted. "Yes, the chemist is out in the back room. I'll get him." It was scratch, scratch and scratch until he came to my rescue.

He was an Australian, he was chewing on a sandwich and by now I was openly scratching. The assistant lingered to eavesdrop.

"Have you got anything for crabs, mate?" I asked.

"Yeah mate, I call it crab fat." Filling a small jar with grey gunk he grinned. "This stuff works a treat mate, no need to shave the family jewels."

It was scratch, scratch, scratch, all the way back to the ship.

We delivered the *English Star* to a dry dock in North Shields then we were sent back to London to join the *Royal Star*, the oldest ship in the fleet, infested with cockroaches and recently sold to the Greeks. The accommodation was very basic, so too was the food, but I knew that if I survived the next ten days and kept my nose clean I was certain to be asked to join the company. That was my plan.

Leaving London on a midnight tide after a very long day of hard, dirty work, we were disgusted to find a few dried up mutton chops and a small dish of fried potato for our evening meal and nothing else.

A bad-tempered older seaman was livid with what was supposed to be a decent meal for twelve hungry men. The food had been put out for us too early and had been attacked by the dockers before they left the ship and while we were busy working.

Finding a cigarette butt in the now congealed potato was the straw that broke the camel's back. He blew his top. Ranting and raving like an old style union rabble-rouser, he soon had us fired up into a belligerent, angry rabble.

"Right lads, who's coming with me to show this rubbish to the skipper?"

I volunteered without hesitation. Full of fury he stomped his way up the companionways to the bridge with the dish of potato with me hot on his heels in support. Once on the bridge a junior mate emerged from the darkness and asked what we were doing on the bridge without permission.

My hero loudly demanded to see the captain who eventually came out of the black wheelhouse and listened to the complaint. A torch shone on the dish highlighting the large roll-your-own cigarette butt.

"Look at this, will you?"

The Captain snorted, casually tossed the butt into the Thames below and demanded a spoon. One appeared in a flash. With the dish under his chin the Skipper wolfed down four spoons of our potato, burped and stated: "There's nothing wrong with it."

The sailor lost control. "You've just eaten half our bloody dinner, you hungry bastard," he screamed. Our names were recorded; we were ordered from the bridge back to our quarters and were the only two seamen not offered positions with the company.

That was the end of my Blue Star experience.

Blisworth

Blisworth

The General Steamship Company had many ships around the British coast that also went to minor Mediterranean and continental ports. They were all small ships, favoured by married seaman wanting to stay close to home.

The *Blisworth* was one of them, only seven hundred and thirty-four tons, with a total crew of fourteen men, everything about her was small and manageable.

When I joined her in St. Katherine's Dock on a fine September day in 1959 I had to climb down the gangway to get aboard. Compared with the *Highland Monarch* she was a miniature and we worked four hours on, four hours off (another first). I was used to the normal four hours on, eight hours off, but quickly adjusted to the new regime.

With a general cargo we headed down the Thames, through a restless English Channel heading for Portugal and ran into a force-eight gale in the Bay of Biscay. Tossed like a cork in a washing machine, the tiny ship violently pitched, rolled and plunged her gallant bow into huge black shuddering waves. We were atop a wave one moment then plummeting into a massive black hole in another. Sleep was impossible.

Midnight and my watch arrived, but getting to the tiny wheelhouse was another story. Dressed in oilskins, sou'wester and sea boots I was not at my agile best, so dodging waves breaking over the slippery, heaving deck was a life-threatening ordeal. It was with much relief that I burst into the damp wheelhouse surrounded by a blast of salty spray.

I was excited to be in charge as I grabbed the worn wooden wheel. The cheerful Welsh skipper, huddled in a dufflecoat at the spinning clear-view screen, calmly whistled sea shanties. Each time we rode a wave the whistle blew loudly because the lanyard had shrunk in the wet until it was knifed by an unknown hand and silenced.

We battled the black seas through the night until eventually we rounded Cape Finisterre into calmer seas and sailed into the picture-postcard port of Oporto. Walking the sunny streets among the cheerful, leathery-faced locals all in neatly patched denims and black berets, I soon found myself in a small café/bar with girls and music.

Maria was about 25 years old, and said she would look after me while I was in port. Pert, elfin with long dark hair and lively brown eyes, she looked like a cat with red claws and very soon her hand was in mine and I was hers. My basic Spanish mixed with her reasonable English ensured good understanding when she took me home to meet her family before taking me to bed.

It took us a week to load a cargo of huge casks of undiluted port destined for Bristol from the carts pulled by donkeys. With a heavy heart I hauled the last mooring rope aboard; Maria was nowhere in sight.

Although I told myself that she would be as broken-hearted as I was, my cabin mate assured me that she would be back in the bar with another sailor from the ship that had just docked.

While we lashed and secured the oak barrels for the homeward trip, a sailor and the cook appeared with a hand drill, a bicycle pump and four flagons from a hidden spot. The flagons were quickly filled then transferred to the crew's cabins so efficiently it must have been done many times.

But the next day there was chaos. The cook and steward who shared a cabin were from the same small Scottish village. They had both been on the *Blisworth* for nearly a year. Battened down in their cabin with one of the flagons, a bucket, and a pile of sandwiches, they also had the keys to the galley and food locker.

Through the night they sang strange Gaelic songs, laughing raucously, and were still at it in the morning when the skipper arrived. Using their Christian names, he pleaded on his knees through the air vent in the door. It was a comical sight.

The singing was softer, the pleading more plaintive, and even the threat of dismissal was met with slurred, salty vocabulary. While a crowbar opened the food locker, a hacksaw freed the galley padlock; loaves of bread, bacon, eggs and tins of beans were handed out and the crisis was over. The singing finally ceased in the wee small hours.

As we sailed back across the bay in the autumn sunshine things returned to normal. The cook and steward were back at their posts as if nothing had happened. Less than a month after leaving London we passed under the old Bristol bridge and docked at an ancient pier, where many a ship with similar men had delivered similar cargoes many times before.

m.s. "VALDES" - Mac Andrew Line - U.K./Spain.   16656

Valdes

MacAndrews Line was a small, well-respected shipping company on the Mediterranean run. I was lucky as it was hard to get a job on MacAndrews Line ships because the conditions and food were so good crews never left. MacAndrews was also known as the Polish Navy.

Five years my senior, Pete was the other AB who was sent with me to join the MS *Valdes* in Surrey Docks on a chilly November day in 1959. To my surprise Pete demanded a taxi and was granted one. Pete knew the ropes and took charge of everything and I automatically followed him.

Pete was a short, stocky, bellicose East Ender who spoke mostly in rhyming slang. He informed me that Valdes was some Spanish geezer from olden days. Pete did not like Jam Rolls (Polish people). This ship was full of them. According to Pete, even the Sheriff (Boatswain) and two Ginger Beers (Engineers) were Jam Rolls. Pete, grumpy from the start, was dreading having to share a cabin with a Jam Roll.

German built, the *Valdes* was similar to the *Baltic Express*, very streamlined with comfortable accommodation. Much to his relief, Pete and I shared a cabin and were put on the graveyard watch: 12–4am, 12–4pm.

The food was excellent. The cook had married a company director's daughter and personally ordered the stores for each voyage. He was also earmarked for a chef's job at the famous Dorchester Hotel. He had standards to maintain and we were fed royally. To have a crab or lobster entrée served in large scallop shells was unheard of in a crew mess room of the British Merchant Navy in the fifties.

At meal times the cook would proudly present the dish personally and await our reactions with a beaming smile. He also had a smattering of Polish greetings to keep the Jam Rolls happy. Pete didn't trust the Babbling Brook (the cook) because of this. Pete enjoyed the food without praise, unlike the Jam Rolls who were just toady lickspittles in Pete's eyes. They weren't British. They were taking British seamen's jobs. British seamen had fought long and hard for these conditions. There was always tension in the air whenever a Jam Roll was near Pete.

Ashore in Gibraltar, we climbed the Rock to see the apes that all looked like Jam Rolls according to Pete. We sailed into the small Spanish ports of Malaga, Cartagena, Alicante and Valencia, unloading general cargo and loading crates of oranges, olive oil and sardines. Pete was looking forward to Barcelona, his favorite port it was where he had a squeeze (girlfriend). I was pleased that Pete was happy at last. Sadly, it was a short-lived happiness.

On arrival, Pete let out a stream of salty invective because Barcelona was now home to the American Fleet. All the boozers would be crammed with Ham Shanks (Yanks). The Jam Rolls smirked at Pete's misfortune.

Their interest was the nearest bodega while ours was the nearest bordello.

We took to the back streets and found a bar without Yanks. Pete's squeeze arrived with a friend then within an hour we were both being accommodated in a hotel with mirrored rooms and mirrored ceilings. Too quickly, Pete was banging on the door with a bottle of brandy while the ladies were eager to return to the bar for the next customers.

Later that evening a drunken Pete was ejected onto the street and for the first time I took charge of him and got him safely back to the ship. With effort, Pete staggered up the gangway watched by a sniggering line of Jam Rolls, then, as he stepped aboard he planted a punch on the first Jam Roll in sight.

Unfortunately, it was the sober night watchman just doing his job. We were both fined, put in the logbook then on arrival back in London we were both replaced by two Polish deck-hands.

Pete left *Valdes* just as he joined it. Muttering about Jam Rolls.

Amazon (artist's impression)

Amazon in reality (a working girl)

The Amazon

"Great Steamers white and gold go rolling down to Rio."

In January 1960 I joined the *Amazon* on its maiden voyage to South America. Built by Harland & Woolf in Belfast, she was fully air-conditioned for both passengers and crew. She was also painted white and gold. With her sister ships *Aragon* and *Arlanza* nearing completion, the three sisters were the replacements to the aged but much loved *Highland Monarch, Highland Brigade, Highland Princess* and the *Highland Chieftain.*

The British Seamen's Union had negotiated with the company to employ many local Belfast men as crew to assist the city's unemployment problem.

The deck-hands were an interesting bunch of old timers and youngsters my age, just happy to be at sea, while the cooks, stewards and officers were company men from the Highland boats. In charge of all this was the senior Company Captain. Commodore Sang always wore a broad smile and his Sunday-best, laden with braid. Things ran very smoothly aboard Amazon.

Entering and leaving ports on a maiden voyage was always a gala occasion with flags and colourful bunting flown from bow to stern.

Las Palmas was our first port on our first trip. A huge floral tribute on the dock wall read *"Bienvenido Amazon"* with British and the Spanish flags displayed above a civic band with a brightly dressed bandmaster waving his white-gloved hands in time to the music. Girls in traditional dress swirled, clacked their castanets and clicked their high-heeled boots in time to strumming guitars. Senoritas draped many garlands around the beaming Commodore's neck while a high official placed a kiss on both his rosy cheeks.

The press and passengers took photographs while a tug squirted a water stream and all ships sounded their horns. It was very festive, the traders were kept away and crew shore leave was forbidden. Finally with the band playing "Rule

Britannia" we sailed with more siren blasts and another squirt from the tug.
tug.

A wall of flowers for Amazon at Las Palmas

We put away the flags and bunting and headed for Brazil. Social life aboard was excellent. The crew bar (Pig and Whistle) was the centre of attraction and always busy. Ice cold McEwans beer was a superb treat at the end of a day's toil in the tropics. Sailors and engine oilers mixed with kitchen hands, laundrymen, cooks, stewards, cleaners, bottle washers and some whose jobs we never knew.

The beefy barman and baggage master controlled the Crown & Anchor game that went on into the early hours of each day. They were reputed to be very wealthy men and always shadowed by a very large ex-Marine commando when the money was on the table.

The bosun was one of the biggest men aboard. He had a face that spoke of many battles and ran the crew with an iron fist. He knew exactly who'd had too much beer at the lunchtime session in the Pig and Whistle.

Some of the Belfast boys constantly fought among themselves when drunk. The leader of the Protestants was a crude, strident type with some status in his local Orange Lodge back in Belfast. One day he decided to push his luck with the bosun by refusing to turn out for work. No one knew what took place in the empty cabin but he emerged bleeding and apologetic. The Belfast boys stopped fighting after that day.

Author (3rd from right) with "The Belfast Boys"

Crossing the Equator ceremony was a day of well-organised fun for the passengers around the swimming pool. A bearded King Neptune with trident dealt out punishment to all first timers who were smeared with a cocktail of waste food slops, grease and paint, then dumped into the pool at Neptune's nod. A certificate was awarded to all participants. The ceremony ended with another nod from Neptune, a signal for our gang of cleaners to be set upon and thrown fully clothed into the pool by a group of shrieking near-naked females. In the mêlée, my imagination had me believing that a small soft hand had fondled my genitalia just before I hit the slimy water.

Later that evening a concert was held in the stewards' mess room. Two bulky stewards with wigs and lipstick checked crew invitations at the door. Commodore Sang was guest of honour with a personal entourage of first class passengers and fellow officers with gold glitter to match the ladies.

The mess room had been transformed into a nightclub with a stage, coloured lights and crepe paper to successfully soften the stark clean bulkheads. All lights were dimmed for the entrance of "The Sugar Plum Fairy", an obese, sweating laundryman with a wand and missing dentures who opened the show with risqué jokes just clean enough for the Commodore's guests. A mermaid on a papier-mâché reef observed the Amazon's passing through huge binoculars and quipped about the lack of any men aboard.

"Ooh, look there's three on the top deck. Aah, sadly they are just officers." It was pure pantomime that had the packed messroom erupting with laughter.

The skits and dialogues were hilarious. The plump and the painted primped, lisped and camped their way through two hours of semi-prepared nonsense that had the Commodore clutching his ample midriff. The show was a resounding success that kept the ship talking for days.

Arrival in Rio was another festival of flowers, flags, fireworks, bunting, klaxons and bands with dancing dusky maidens all creating a wonderful sight. In Montevideo there was another multi-coloured musical party welcome and departure before Buenos Aires turned out its Blue and White best with me hoping that Laughing Loretta would be free for me that night.

It was to be our last time together. She was to marry an American naval officer and going to live on the family ranch in Texas. Sadness for me with happiness for her was a strange mix. Buenos Aires would never be the same without Loretta.

The voyage back to England had an added excitement for the crew with the antics of an exquisite English girl of fifteen years who strode the decks in a bikini. She was very aware that every red-blooded male aboard openly ogled or furtively eyed her. Her parents were in despair at her overt flirting behaviour while she relished her temporary power. Her nickname was Lolita. She was a much-desired nymphet who was discussed with ribald and licentious interest among the crew.

By the time we reached England Lolita had found romance with a handsome first trip bellboy. She was pregnant. He never got to enjoy another trip to sea. His life had been permanently altered by a burst of passion on a warm night at sea.

It was a fitting end for a maiden voyage.

Andes

A Trip with Bob

My second trip on the *Amazon* was just prior to my twenty-first birthday and I was eager to be back at sea again. There were many new faces among the crew. The Belfast boys had gone back to their green or orange enclaves. I would miss their humour and frequent fighting.

Back in my original cabin I found my new cabin mate, thirty-year old Bob, already settled in and stretched out on the favoured top bunk. He ignored my outstretched hand of greeting with a grunt.

My heart sank a little at this odd behaviour, but I chose to accept his moodiness as a short-term thing. Perhaps he was a married man with children, not as enthusiastic as I was to be outward bound.

Maybe he had stomach ulcers, perhaps haemorrhoids; many seamen suffered with both of them. After a few days at sea things would improve.

But alas, it wasn't to be. Bob turned out to be a moody, fussy control freak who treated me like a young whippersnapper intruding on his personal space.

When Bob wanted the porthole open or shut there was no discussion to be had. When Bob wanted the light on or off he was in charge of the switch. There was no reading under my bunk light when Bob wanted his shuteye.

No shipmates came to the cabin for a chinwag or game of cribbage and no one wanted to swap cabins with me. I was in a prison cell with the jailer and it was very uncomfortable.

Day after day, Bob nagged and nagged while I stewed with pent-up anger. Everything I did was met with tut-tut sounds and anything I said was cut short with a curt retort. He was older and I knew nothing.

I kept out of the 12x6-foot cabin as much as possible but I knew something had to be done about the situation. A volcano was brewing within me.

The day finally came when I snapped and deliberately slammed my mug of tea down on the pristine, constantly cleaned Formica desktop. The frilly paper mat that Bob insisted I use was saturated.

It was High Noon on the High Seas.

Bob flew into a red-faced rage as I knew he would. Screaming obscenities through spittle and quivering lips, Bob ordered me "On Deck."

I followed him with a feverish eagerness.

The fight, in front of midday sunbathers and bridge officers doing their sextant readings, was very brief. Bob was no fighter. He fell under a flurry of uncontrolled punches.

There was blood on the deck and I felt really good about it. However, I still had to share that cabin with Bob for the rest of the voyage. Bob never uttered another word to me from that moment on.

It was now Bob who stayed out of the cabin and I who had control of the light switch and porthole, but I was glad to see the end of that voyage and the back of Bob.

Highland Chieftain

Highland Chieftain at the end

"ARLANZA"—20,000 TONS GROSS.
Royal Mail Lines' passenger service between United Kingdom, France, Spain, Portugal, Canary Islands, Brazil, Uruguay and Argentina.

Arlanza and Aragon, sister ships of the Amazon

"ARAGON"—20,000 TONS GROSS.
Royal Mail Lines' passenger service between United Kingdom, France, Spain, Portugal, Canary Islands, Brazil, Uruguay and Argentina.

Adios Amazon

After zipping about London on a Lambretta scooter dressed Italian, rocking and rolling with Valerie, for the first time I was reluctant to sail but I rejoined *Amazon* for another trip.

Again through the crowded docks, in the wonderful hubbub of London at its best; through the ancient swing bridge and locks, down river to Tilbury to embark new passengers for South America on *Amazon* voyage No 3.

The bosun now used my Christian name and promoted me to deckman in charge of passengers, quoits, pucks, mallets and other games. I was also responsible for the upkeep of all wooden doors on all passenger decks. It was a fantastic job. I had landed the much coveted "Varnish King's" job and I was allowed to speak with passengers when spoken to.

Heading for Brazil I was required for horse racing evenings to move the numbered wooden horses however many places their dice was thrown. Observing from the sidelines on dance nights I noted that smiling Commodore Sang was an excellent dancer, light on his feet and in constant demand as he twirled the ladies to the sounds of Victor Sou'wester and his Ballroom Raindrops played on a gramophone. There was no rock and roll at these dances.

As we berthed on arrival in Rio a gust of wind took hold of our bow, pulling us away from the pier. Urgent orders flew from the bosun for extra turns quickly applied to the bollards to arrest the swing. Suddenly a rope parted with a loud crack and snaked through the fairlead with terrifying speed, wrapping around the bosun's leg, felling him with a thud then dragging him like a rag doll towards the gaping hole in the bow.

Luckily the rope unwrapped from his leg like a fleeing boa constrictor leaving him sitting red-faced but still alive and still on board. It was all over in an instant. A sombre silence hung among us as we realised that even the big, tough, experienced bosun could dramatically slip up sometimes.

With his leg heavily bandaged, he limped through his daily routine with determination while we the crew thought no more of it as we left Rio, arrived and departed Montevideo and entered Buenos Aires a week later.

With marlin spike in hand the bosun reached above his head to tighten a shackle. Suddenly, without warning he fell onto his backside, a blank look on his red face. His massive legs thrashed like a child in a tantrum. Then he slumped flat on his back in front of us. Someone ran for the doctor as the bosun's mate put an ear to the giant chest. On arrival the doctor sent the nurse scampering back with urgent words of instruction.

We stood silently in a semi-circle helpless and mesmerised by the lifeless hulk. The doctor pronounced him dead just as the nurse returned with a small black case, then a liquid was injected into his arm. "Last resort." The doctor's words were casual and calm. It was thought a blood clot from his recent accident had taken a week to travel to his heart, causing a fatal blockage.

Six of us carried him aft to the mortuary and laid him on a shelf. The morgue was heavily littered by the stevedores in Montevideo and needed cleaning. The deck-boy was sent for a broom and left to the task.

Automatically the bosun's mate became bosun. The lamp-trimmer became bosun's mate. A senior able seaman became lamp-trimmer and we all returned to normal routine.

The young deck-boy later told of his absolute terror, left alone with the bosun's body. He worked feverishly, keeping one eye on the colossal corpse only inches away. He was certain that he would have died of fright if the bosun had sat up. The body was flown back to his family in Liverpool.

We sailed past the white cliffs of Dover on an exquisite August day.

After a year on the *Amazon* it was time for another change.

R.M.S. "LOCH GOWAN" 9,718 TONS
Royal Mail Lines' Cargo/Passenger Service between United Kingdom and North Pacific Coast.

Loch Gowan

With just twelve first-class passengers the *Loch Gowan* was unashamedly a cargo ship. I joined her as an AB on a brisk January day in 1961.

Fully laden we headed outward bound for the Panama Canal, the West Coast of America and Vancouver, Canada. Mature silver-haired couples and two recently widowed friends made up the passenger list.

The chief mate was a rough diamond who had started life at sea as a deck boy in the fo'c'sle, not as an officer cadet, and was well respected throughout the Royal Mail Lines fleet. He could splice, and swear as well as any man aboard. He had been mate for many years. This was his ship and he knew every rivet from bow to stern. He loved his job but hated wearing a uniform. He wore his cap only when rank needed to be displayed.

Once in warmer climes a basic swimming pool was assembled on deck then filled with a hose from a hydrant for the ladies to bobble about in.

The mate lived up to his reputation in Panama while supervising the lowering of the gangway from an upper deck.

The gangway jammed halfway down. A kink in a rope had foiled the precise operation that was meant to impress the ladies in the audience.

"Get that fucking gangway down now," he bellowed. An officer cadet was hurriedly dispatched by the skipper to remind the mate that there were "Ladies aboard." The youth was loudly blasted with a riposte from the irate mate.

"Well if they're fucking ladies they won't understand a fucking word, will they?"

The smirking ladies were not shocked.

We sailed through the Canal in a spectacular tropical rainstorm. Thunder rumbled low overhead while lightning fizzed, hissed and crackled all about. The sky turned black. For a while day was turned into night. Then just a few hours later we were heading north through glassy Pacific seas abundant with marine life.

Flying fish flashed across the surface pursued by porpoises. Turtles lolled on the waves and tuna skipped. Pelicans dove into schools of fish, surfaced with full wriggling pouches then expertly flipped the catch down their gullets headfirst. We saw one feeding pelican vanish before our eyes into the jaws of a large brown shark.

Early morning arrival at the Port of San Diego was a fantastic experience. We were efficiently escorted to a berth across the harbour from an enormous aircraft carrier surrounded by a fleet of naval ships. Destroyers, submarines, landing craft and fast patrol boats were everywhere. Navy jets practiced take-off drills all day. The booming, roaring noise was constant. Tugs tooted, railway wagons banged and clanged, whistles blew, and bells rang. The clamour was wonderfully energizing. Several MG, TD and TF Sports cars belonging to returning soldiers were the first things landed. The boss of the Waterside Workers' Union was the proud father of a returning son.

Our next port of call was Long Beach just a bus ride away from Los Angeles and perhaps a chance to see famous places like Pasadena, Santa Barbara and others places heard in cowboy movies and songs.

Three of us headed ashore along the long dusty road to the bus stop and town. A buxom middle-aged blonde in a bright red convertible with tailfins and copious chrome swished to a stop.

"You boys wanna ride?" We gleefully piled in, two in the back and me in the front. Jackie Wilson warbled 'Reet Petit' from the chrome radio. We tapped our toes and cooed at the opulence.

While admiring the tinted wraparound windscreen a jewelled hand squeezed my knee. "Have you a harrrrd-on?" The ringed fingers crept higher. My shipmates lounging on the back seat were totally oblivious to the happenings in the front. On arrival she handed me a business card. "Gloria Anytime" with a phone number. We laughed a lot that day, trotting around L.A.

One Sunday morning we idly observed a long green station wagon drive along the deserted wharf and come to a stop at our gangway. Out tumbled a stocky Scotsman with a heavy Glasgow accent. Then his even stockier teenage son followed with an American accent. The nostalgic father had read the *Shipping News* and brought his son to visit M.V. *Loch Gowan* assuming the crew would all be Scotsmen too.

Alas, we were all Londoners. But, welcomed aboard for a pot of tea they in turn invited us to their Church Hall Dance. There I danced with a perky girl with blonde pigtails, a flared skirt and white socks who decided to take me home to meet Mommy and Daddy. The Senior Scotsman gave me a sober warning to behave as I departed.

Mommy, knitting in an armchair watching TV, was not very friendly. Her piercing blue eyes studied me coldly over glittering spectacles as she continued to knit baby boots. Her probing questions were hostile and edgy.

Later, a car pulled into the driveway. Pigtails skipped excitedly to the door. "Hi Daddy, this is a sailor from London, England." Daddy was a big man with a florid face and lantern jaw. He strode past without a glance at Mommy, Pigtails or me. "You've got five minutes to get outta here," he growled. I was left with an outstretched hand. Pigtails ran to her room in tears.

I found myself on a strange street looking for a taxicab to take me away from the famous American hospitality.

San Francisco was another unforgettable occasion. Sailing past the famous Alcatraz Prison and under the Golden Gate Bridge was a thrill for a London lad, never to be forgotten. The amazing trams defied gravity as they hurtled around the hills, clanging their bells. I spent a whole day without a destination just for the fun and a hope that I might meet Judy Garland.

Aboard Loch Gowan under the Golden Gate bridge

Vancouver was a pleasant place where we loaded huge tree trunks in the lower holds and cartons of salmon and ham in the 'tween decks. Sailing south to Seattle through the sounds, dwarfed by mountains and forests high above us, was Wild West America.

Once ashore, we went to a rustic eating place for a breakfast of hash browns, rashers of streaky bacon, eggs sunny side up, mountains of toast buttered with a paintbrush, followed by pancakes with maple syrup, all washed down with help-yourself coffee. It was easily the biggest breakfast I'd ever eaten. I could hardly move so I sat satisfied, observing our surroundings.

The locals were dressed in dungarees, boots, thick brightly coloured shirts, fringed buckskin jackets and cowboy hats. Davy Crockett would easily fit in here.

Back in Long Beach the blonde in the red convertible was again offering lifts into town. The Scottish family welcomed us like old friends and bade us farewell when we sailed with huge tree trunks chained to our decks.

Back through the Panama, with tins of salmon and ham supplementing our normal rations on the homeward run we were a happy crew. Rigging repairs and maintenance was attended to. Washing and painting the ship from top to toe in perfect tropical weather was never a chore.

We arrived back in London with a happy Chief Mate pleased with his crew and proud of his freshly painted ship. As we entered the docks a voice called from a nearby ship.

"Are there any Geordies aboard?" The time-honoured reply came floating back.

"No, we're all white men aboard here."

I was home on a wave of laughter.

Lotus Cortina Mk II (not bought from Arthur Daley)

Landlubber

In the summer of 1961 I went ashore and lived with a family who ran a corner shop in Camberwell, south-east London.

The crammed, tiny shop sold everything. Newspapers, cigarettes, lemonade, ice creams, tea, sugar, coffee, soap, bootlaces, cheese, balls of string, baked beans, candles, balloons, butter and snuff for the old men and some women. The assortment of smells was a delight.

I used snuff with my detective friend who carried his in a waistcoat pocket and employed a very precise procedure when indulging. A couple of good sneezes cleared the brain he'd say, but he never sneezed.

Behind the shop was a living room also used as a storeroom for cartons of cigarettes and sundry goods awaiting shelf room in the shop. A net curtain on the dividing glass door allowed us to observe the arrival of customers. As they entered the shop bell would clang loudly. At times it rang nonstop.

A long passageway also used for storage included a wash basin and cooking stove and led to a small yard where the toilet was housed.

The yard was also home to many stacked crates of empty bottles and a German shepherd guard dog whose sole purpose was to constantly bark at arrogant cats on the surrounding high walls and deposit droppings everywhere in the limited space. A night time visit to the yard required a torch and careful step.

Fred and Irene, their two sons and I slept in just two bedrooms above the shop while under the beds, boxes of chocolates were stored.

With no bath, bathing was best done at local Municipal Public Baths where for a few shillings you could lie up to your neck in a deep bath of hot water in one of the cubicles. A call for more hot water in Number 22 would bring the white-clad attendant along the corridor with his brass turnkey. Another voice requested the same in number 15. Sounds of satisfaction and splashing bodies filled the air in the steamy, tiled cavernous space. Regular visits and many hours of relaxation were enjoyed there.

One day, Irene's younger sister arrived from Lincoln with her two baby daughters for a London holiday. How eight of us fitted into the already congested quarters was a miracle but certainly not an unpleasant experience. There was constant laughter and amusement.

I worked for a local bakery delivering bread in an electric van with a top speed of seven miles per hour. I earned good commission on all cakes and biscuits I sold. My patch was around the Old Kent Road area.

The cheeky kids on the estates would regularly hang from the rubbing strakes on the slow moving van watched by their laughing mothers from the balconies above.

It was an entertaining break for my housebound customers, until one day, with the sides full of laughing brats, I wound the van up to full speed then stamped down hard on the brakes. The kids fell from the van with shrieks of laughter. I was now immobile and going nowhere; my brakes had seized.

On my return from a nearby phone box, I found the van doors wide open, my stock gone. A scattering of loose buns pointed to the exits. My large wicker basket was missing and there was not a kid in sight. Feeling like a character in a comic book scene, I ranted about calling the police to no avail. Invisible childish laughter was loud and derisive. My boss was not amused however, and my employment was terminated on my late arrival back at the depot.

Shortly after that incident my name reached the top of the waiting list for the Royal Mail Lines Shore Gang. It was good to be working on ships again, shifting empty vessels between different docks, loading stores, removing engine parts and cleaning holds between cargoes.

No one in the gang relished cleaning the fertilizer ships and taking the smell home. The 'Sugar Boats' were much preferred. They were sticky but far less odorous. Most of the gangs were ex-seamen with families to support, with the exception of one beefy East Ender who carried a small axe tucked down his belt and constantly looked over his shoulder.

He was from a large family of dockers who had a longstanding vendetta with another East End gang. Two of his brothers were serving long stretches in Wormwood Scrubs Prison for armed robbery and G.B.H. (grievous bodily harm)

In the London docks you saw nuffin', heard nuffin' and said nuffin'.

The Shore Gangs Annual Picnic was on a hot August day. We assembled in a dockside pub at 7am where the beer was already flowing when I arrived, the boys already rowdy.

Crates of beer were stacked along the aisle of the bus before we took to the road for a trip to Clacton-on-sea. Another bus behind us was full of partying women from a local factory also on a day trip to Clacton.

It wasn't long before one of our lads gave the ladies a 'browneye' through the rear window. Far from embarrassed, the ladies clapped their encouragement until a line of buttocks lined the window. Regular roadside comfort stops had the ladies squatting in bushes and the lads squirting the rear wheel of the bus, plus getting acquainted.

A few of us walked the beach taking in the sea air while the rest united in song with the factory girls in a seafront pub. The late evening return trip was less boisterous with tired bodies weakly singing half-remembered songs amid some snoring.

I was relieved when the long day of male bonding and boozing was over. An early morning start the following day was the focus. Another ship was arriving. Long hours of hard, dirty work didn't deter us from working overtime through the warm nights, often till daybreak. Good money was earned.

Eventually, with winter on the horizon, my mind was on Australia. Easing another departing ship out on a midnight tide the pilot called to the tug's skipper. "Keep her off the knuckle Harry." It was a clarion call to me.

I was ready for another splash of salt spray.

Orcades, P&O Line

POSH P & O

Port Outward—Starboard Homeward.

The P & O liner *Orcades* was homeward bound and heading for Southampton when I strode into their office looking for employment in November 1961. These were magical days when a seaman could pick and choose which shipping company to offer his labour to, choose whatever part of the globe to head for and, with good timing, avoid another winter.

I was sent with a group of others by train to Southampton to deliver a beautiful old liner named *Orontes* to Tilbury docks. She had been sold for scrap. Our job was to remove the ship's stores, fittings and equipment to local warehouses. Carpets, curtains, bedding, pots and pans, ropes and paint, everything went ashore on the backs and shoulders of many men. For days I was a worker ant in an endless chain, ruefully dismantling 32 years of accumulated maritime history. One quiet lunchtime I spotted crates of silver cutlery and chandeliers from the saloons disappear into the waiting vehicles of a group of smartly dressed gentlemen waving wads of cash.

Eventually *Orcades* arrived with great excitement. Hundreds of people crammed the pier while tanned colonial passengers seemed unaware of the winter drizzle. I quickly settled back into shipboard routine aboard *Orcades* although crammed into a cabin with eight bunks, eight tin lockers, a wooden table, two benches for seating, one porthole and seven other deckhands. Finally *Orcades* sailed for Suez past the sad skeleton of *Orontes* with its two raked woodbine funnels finally breathless and finished with engines.

Gold braid and uniforms were abundant and a no-nonsense boatswain ensured things ran with military precision aboard *Orcades*. We visited Lisbon, Gibraltar and Naples then cleared the Suez Canal one black night into the Red Sea for Aden and the long leg to Fremantle, Western Australia.

It was a night to remember. Sharing a beer and chat with cabin mates, the ambience was shattered when a large, drunken Scotsman named Angus crashed through our cabin door. He began yelling at Duncan, half his size. They were both from Aberdeen and Duncan had enjoyed the company of Angus's young sister on his last shore leave. Things were very tense in the small space and reasoning with the angry bull proved futile.

Standing in front of a seated Duncan, Angus suddenly grabbed his hair and slammed his knee into Duncan's nose with a sickening crunch. Blood spurted as Duncan fell to the deck unconscious. There was instant bedlam.

Paul from the Hebrides threw the first punch, which sent Angus flying against the bulkhead. Then in a flash he speared a long bench at his head. Angus ducked just in time. Beer mugs smashed against bunks and the cabin deck was like an ice rink, awash with beer and blood. Paul and I were the only willing opponents to the thrashing Angus. While I was riding the back of the raging bull, another punch from Paul sent me crashing among the beer, blood and broken glass and I saw stars.

In the melée I heard a high-pitched scream I thought was a woman and noticed the others fleeing the cabin as Angus punched Paul into a corner.

I found myself with a knife in one hand and an ear in the other ready to slice. But I lost my footing. Four frustrated slashes across his back were enough to bring Angus to his senses. He'd had enough.

We threw the bleeding Angus out of the cabin into the arms of the Master-at-Arms and his Mate. There were threats of death over his shoulder as he was marched away. The screaming cowards cleaned the cabin while we cleaned Duncan and ourselves.

Fear, anger and excitement merged into a feeling of pleasure and satisfaction that kept me from sleep that night. But it could have been worse. It could have been manslaughter. The next morning, we were escorted to the Commander's Office by the Boatswain to explain ourselves.

We all had cuts and battle scars. I sported a black eye. Paul sported two. Duncan with a broken nose, swollen lips and eyes two purple slits, was a mess. Angus, now stitched and fully clothed, displayed the least damage as he towered over the battered Duncan.

Threatened with prison in Australia for another indiscretion, Angus became a polite and sober crewmember for the rest of the voyage.

Flashy in Hawaii

An Australian Accountant

"You simply must visit Lionel in Australia." It was more of a direction from the friendly matron I'd met on my last shore leave. Her only brother had gone to Australia after the war. "You simply must." I sent a letter warning of my impending arrival in Melbourne aboard *Orcades*.

In Fremantle Australia I received a brief note from Lionel. A car would meet me on arrival in Port Melbourne. I arranged a day off.

My Irish Catholic upbringing urged that I always present myself at my best when meeting new and possibly important people. Once berthed in Melbourne I grabbed a shower and shave then, back in my cabin I broke out my new, navy blue English suit.

I donned a double cuff dress shirt and clipped on my chrome and blue cut glass American cufflinks. A matching tie-pin held my blue silk tie in place. Winklepicker zip-up boots were buffed. A fake folded handkerchief on a card was slotted into the breast pocket of my bumfreezer jacket. Splashes of Old Spice aftershave were applied and I was ready. I felt and looked like a tailor shop dummy. "Blimey mate, you look like a pox doctor's clerk and smell like a Spanish brothel."

The gangway man dressed in shorts and T-shirt announced my visitor's arrival. I followed him outside to the crew gangway where the fierce midday heat and a chorus of wolf whistles greeted me. A smiling, portly man in his fifties stepped from the gangway with an outstretched hand. It was Lionel. He was dressed in baggy grey shorts and a green paint-spattered tennis shirt. Unbuckled sandals jingled on his bare feet. I was overdressed and already sweating profusely, so I suggested to Lionel that I pop back to my cabin to change into something more casual.

With a twinkle in his eye and a chuckle in his voice Lionel insisted that I was perfectly dressed. Just perfect! A battered Morris Minor with windows down soon had us rattling along a hot seafront road on the way to Lionel's house, I presumed. Instead, we swung into the crowded car park of the Black Rock Hotel and came to a dusty stop under a tree. Lionel insisted I keep my jacket and tie on and hurried me into the cool, dark interior.

It seemed that everyone greeted chuckling Lionel as we made our way to the bar. Battered hats, boots, shorts and singlets were the mode of dress here and I stood out like a sore thumb. Lionel explained to one of his mates that I was "From England".

"You could have bloody fooled me, mate," was the dry reply.

The smell of beer, body odour and cigarette smoke soon smothered the aftershave. With loosened tie and minus my jacket I was cooler and more relaxed but the glittering cufflinks were still like a swinging watch to the hypnotized drinkers. I was being pointed out to all newcomers. A collective guffaw followed: "Who's your girlfriend, Lionel?"

Halfway through my second glass of chilled beer, a skinny toothless drunk with leathery skin and toweling hat appeared at my elbow, eyeing me slowly from top to toe like a pantomime character. There was an unnatural quiet as this obvious pub clown lined me up for his captive audience.

"Are you a poofter, mate?"

I heard sniggers and glanced at Lionel surrounded by grinning mates, then held one watery marbled eyeball with a long silence. I deliberately and theatrically looked him up and down in return and heard a pin drop. Mimicking his nasal Australian drawl, I replied: "Naw mate. Are you?"

The bar erupted into laughter as he sheepishly lurched toward the urinal. Lionel and I were backslapped and treated to another beer. I had broken the Aussie ice.

Later, the drunk shook my hand and drawled from the side of his mouth.

"You're all right for a bloody POM."

Lionel's restraining hand assured me it was meant as a compliment.

Later, I met with Lionel's family. I was fed and fussed over then delivered back to the floodlit *Orcades* for the trip to Sydney.

Melbourne was a wonderful memory. Who said accountants were boring?

The Bunch of Grapes

The *Orcades* was always referred to by its name only. At noon *Orcades* had sailed X amount of nautical miles. *Orcades* ETA in the port of Sydney would be X time. On the port side of *Orcades* a pod of whales could be observed. *Orcades* winning Bingo numbers were. Blah. Blah. Blah.

On a sparkling Australian summer morning, the towering mast of *Orcades* slid under the massive Harbour Bridge and Sydney seduced me. The bustling harbour was a memorable sight; a huge armada of vessels from liners, cargo ships, ferries, tugs, boats and yachts, all with a purpose.

Everything about *Orcade*s was feverishly well organised on our arrival in Sydney. The gold braid gleamed and the white was crisply starched.

Sydney was considered the ultimate in P & O "showtime" in the Colonies. The gangways went down with military precision as strutting uniforms passed orders to everyone in sight. Delighted women screamed.

An ice-cold Aussie beer on a hot Aussie day is an exquisite pleasure and should be compulsory, said an Australian shipmate. Scrubbed and cleaned, a group of us headed ashore for some fun. Luna Park Fairground was ticked off the list with the next stop the renowned Sydney Pub "The Bunch of Grapes."

Seamen preferred the name "The Bunch of C---s"; a crude reference to female genitalia. I'd heard many good yarns about "The Bunch" – now it was time to experience it for myself.

Six of us found a stand-up table by the door and surveyed our surroundings while we indulged. All nationalities and professions filled the bar with a wonderful hubbub of happy sound. A bunch of raucous, well oiled Aussie Navy boys had a similar table by the toilets and were hovering on the dangerous ridge of happiness and malice. They had obviously been there for a while.

Later, one of our boys returned from the urinal with a frown. An Aussie had stuck a foot out and tripped him as he emerged from having a piss and "Pommie Bastard" was heard among the laughter.

We were Irish, Scots and English with obvious regional accents and no doubt the overseas gentlemen being referred to. A second trip was unsuccessful, but by now, taunts and tensions were in the air. We muttered and drank and drank and muttered and then we got drunk. They eyeballed us and we eyeballed them back.

Something had to happen.

There were seven of them and six of us, all about the same size. I had a plan.

With lowered tones, I hatched my plan within the circled elbows of my shipmates. "I walk over as if heading for a piss and you fellows follow. No Paddy, I didn't say I'd waltz over there. Bloody listen to me. Anyway, I walk over and smack the nearest one in the mouth then we all get stuck into them, right?"

"Yeah, good idea, we're right behind you mate."

I emptied my glass, then headed for the sneering Navy boys and hit the first one as planned. A flurry of fists soon had me back-pedaling and bleeding. I was on my own and got myself a good licking. A large barman grabbed my collar and rushed me through the door onto the darkening street. "I'm sick of you trouble-making Pommie bastards. Piss off and don't come back."

My sheepish shipmates gathered outside to console me as an unmistakable Aussie voice floated through the air. "On yer way, yer Bunch of Cunts."

It was my first visit to Sydney Australia.

Man Overboard

Auckland, New Zealand was humid and shrouded in cloud as we sailed past a dormant volcano named Rangitoto. There was something spiritual about this place.

Ashore in the afternoon I walked the bustling main street, enjoying the Polynesian sounds of busking bands and the different smells. A beautiful young Maori girl greeted me with the widest, happiest smile and walked me back to the dock gate and the waiting *Orcades.* She told me that she liked Pommie seaman. It was a lingering goodbye and, swimming in those deep brown eyes, I knew I'd return to New Zealand.

Our next stop was Honolulu, Hawaii. Energetic hula girls with quivering hips and guitars welcomed *Orcades* and draped passengers with garlands as they landed ashore. They mixed oddly with efficient American uniformed officials with their crew cuts, glistening military boots and all of them chewing on cigars.

Once again the spectacle of American military might and muscle dominated. With a few of the crew I found time to visit the famous surfing beach of Waikiki and hired a large surfboard from a huge Hawaiian.

Frolicking in the surf was energy-sapping fun and eventually I managed to stay upright for one thrilling return to the beach. Satisfied and sunburned we left that evening for Panama and the final leg of this fantastic journey aboard *Orcades*.

One final bizarre event took place in the Bay of Biscay, a sea well renowned for its turmoil and turbulence.

On this March day of 1962 the sea was flat with a long lazy swell. As *Orcades* sliced its way effortlessly homeward the dreaded call was heard at noon. "Man Overboard". It was hurriedly relayed to the bridge.

Immediately, both marker buoys were released from the wings of the bridge, the engine telegraphs clanged instructions to the engineers to prepare to stop the engines. *Orcades'* powerful whistle pierced the air with its urgent

70

coded warning that sent the whole ship into an efficient rehearsed emergency mode.

The huge liner sailed a figure of eight with its wake and headed back to the marker buoys with two rescue boats already prepared at the waterline. The midday meal was forgotten, with passengers, stewards and cooks at the rails to observe the rescue. The sea was littered with a long corridor of life belts thrown from every deck when the call went out.

An older female passenger had opted to wrap up in a deckchair with a book and a sandwich instead of attending lunch in the saloon. She had noticed an agitated first-class barman pacing the deserted deck, she had screamed as he rushed to the railing and hurled himself overboard into the sea far below. The man was spotted by thousands of eyes, vainly trying to hide beneath one of many jettisoned life belts. As the lifeboat approached, he wildly thrashed and tried to swim away but was firmly dragged ranting into the boat, transferred to a straitjacket and the waiting padded cell.

Every deck took its photographs and every porthole framed a jutting head as the lifeboat was winched home. Another boat rounded up the marker buoys and many life belts; floating among them was a beer crate and a deckchair. While this theatre was occurring a loud splash was heard, then a cheer from the sunbathing stewards on the fore deck.

One of them had accepted a dare to dive from the bow, as high as an Olympic diving board. Swimming happily to the boat he acknowledged the applause high above with a wave of his underpants and ignored the frowns from the bridge.

Standing brazenly in the boat with one foot on the gunwale the crotch of his soggy underpants did nothing to hide his hairy appendages from the bemused passengers as the boat was hauled upward past their clicking cameras. With a defiant grin he yelled to the collected heads at the numerous portholes. "Pull your heads in, it looks like a pig boat from Dublin." His seagoing life ended from that moment and he knew it.

The barman had earlier complained to the Chief Steward that people were looking at him while he worked behind the bar. The passenger with the book wondered why the barman had not thrown himself over the side at night in faraway shark-infested waters.

Rangitoto

Rangitoto in cruising colours

Rangitoto

With another enjoyable shore leave under my belt I was eager to get back to sea and return to New Zealand. Ginger Moxley was in charge of manning the New Zealand Shipping Company ships. His desk was cluttered. His phone rang nonstop. His ginger hair was prematurely grey. He signed me on the *Rangitoto* as an AB with a warning to behave. He had an eagle eye and reportedly, an elephant's memory for names and faces of thousands of deckhands. You stayed in Ginger's good books, or you were told to "Sling your hook."

New Zealand was a popular destination for British sailors; many jumped ship to set up with welcoming women; it was like home away from home. It seemed that everyone had family or friends there. A popular joke was that something in the water made the locals very friendly. I shared a cabin with a chubby, flatulent lad from Bristol. On many occasions my sleep would be interrupted by the rattling bunk rails below that were out of rhythm with normal ship's rattles. Barry was finding pleasure with himself.

In the next cabin, Steve a budding musician, played a very pleasant muted saxophone until Panama, where he purchased a special herb to smoke. He claimed it improved his playing, but he giggled a lot, called everyone brother, and everything was "cool man".

He shared with Colin, a short stocky lad who was doing his last trip before settling down ashore to marry his childhood sweetheart. Many photos plastered the bulkhead above his bunk. She was a plain, homely looking girl. Colin would be well matched. He regularly wrote fifteen and twenty page letters, stacking them up for posting in each port. Most of us were pleased to get an occasional letter in an occasional port. Colin would receive a dozen scented ones in every port. He was happy with thoughts that his best friend back home had promised to watch over her on this, his last trip.

Colin's passion was scuba diving. Crammed under his bunk was wet suit, flippers, goggles, weight belts, a spear gun and oxygen bottles. Bob, another AB, was nicknamed "Elvis" because of his uncanny resemblance to the famous singer. The three of us became good friends both aboard and ashore. On our way across the Pacific we spent our spare time repairing the neglected jollyboat for use in Papeete.

By the time we arrived at Tahiti we had caulked and painted the hull, scraped and varnished the woodwork, repaired the sails and rigging with much approval from the bosun.

The passengers headed ashore to explore this fabled, tropical island. Colin read a bundle of numbered, scented letters from his darling then we lowered the little boat into the water, loaded Colin's gear, then sailed to the reef and my first diving experience. Elvis and I, restricted by our snorkels, watched with awe as Colin dove to great depths in crystal clear water with his spear gun primed.

We swam around huge, brightly coloured mushroom corals as big as houses, dispersing large shoals of tropical fish of every hue and colour. This Brixton boy was in a psychedelic wonder world far from home.

Colin's silent signal brought us to an octopus in its coral cave. I couldn't resist trying to capture it with my home made spear. In a flurry of dust and ink it retreated into its hole leaving my spear twisted and useless and me in awe of the power of its pull.

Colin's next signal was a warning to keep our distance from a huge moray eel's jaws protruding from its hole. He disturbed an ugly looking fish on the seabed and swam alongside, stroking its stumpy body with his knife.

Later he informed us that it was the dreaded stonefish with a highly toxic spine behind its dorsal fin. Well camouflaged against the seafloor it was difficult to spot, and stepping on it would bring a painful death.

Satisfied and contented, we sailed back to the ship with a bucket of fish as the passengers returned for the voyage to New Zealand.

The next day we heard that our stewards had gone ashore mob-handed and started a punch up in the local watering hole because the stewards of the *Rangitata* had been severely dealt to a few weeks earlier.

There were many black eyes among stewards. One of them belonged to "Flash".

It was a nickname Elvis had applied to a young waiter on our first meeting because, despite his miniature stature, "Flash" talked tough with a rough cockney accent and a liberal use of comical rhyming slang. But serving the first-class passengers at meal times "Flash" employed a gentle Oxford accent, dressed in pristine white shirts, neatly pressed black trousers and shiny black shoes.

Wearing a shiner like a ripe plum, Flash began the tale of his previous day's exploits, adopting an aggressive, flyweight boxing stance to enhance his filleted version of the melée. Elvis prodded the swollen eye with a grubby finger. "If you're such a hard man, Flash, how did you get this?" he asked. Flash, determined to impress us, replied with an incredulous tone. "ere, I've only hit this geezer, aven't I? And he only ain't gone down, as he? First time I've hit a geezer who ain't gone down. Know what I mean?" Elvis often parroted the statement and it always brought a laugh.

One day there was a flurry of radio messages between our ship and a cargo ship with a very sick crewmember in urgent need of a doctor. The afternoon rendezvous was on a restless, uneven sea with our crowded decks abuzz with excitement. Two ships in the middle of the South Pacific ocean closing to within a mile of each other was a slow motion spectacle to enjoy.

Our ship's doctor clung grimly to the lifeboat as it dipped out of sight into a great hollow of water then re-appeared again on the next wave chugging toward his next patient with six seasoned sailors. All of them miniatures on a huge, moving moat. Alongside the heaving ship the doctor was snatched aboard from the crest of a wave with his bag of tricks.

The patient needed an operation and was expertly lowered into the heaving, bucking lifeboat with superb timing. The doctor's return to the gyrating lifeboat was also spectacular.

On his third attempt, he stepped into the boat a split-second after it plummeted, but luckily landed on top of two of the boat's crew who broke his fall and one of his ribs.

Both vessels resumed their original courses with whistles blowing congratulations and farewell across the water. The doctor was a hero. He had saved a sailor's life.

A mountain of mail awaited Colin in Wellington. It seemed absurd that two-thirds of the deck hands' mail was scented, written with the same flowing hand and addressed to just one man. Colin loved to gloat.

Outside the dock gate the Waterloo Hotel was always busy and became our second home for our days in Wellington. The public bar served flat beer through clear plastic hoses attached to hand-held taps. With money in front of your empty glass the silent barman would refill it as he moved along the line. No words were needed.

Many rheumy eyes watched the clock ticking its way toward closing time as the barmen worked like robots not caring about spillage. This was the famous 6 o'clock swill in operation. It was serious business. All pubs closed for the weekends. Gladstone bags carted flagons of beer to suburban homes on buses and trains. Crates of beer were loaded into cars and taxis for weekend house parties. It was like a bizarre ritual with everyone carting beer around town.

One evening after a movie, two attractive young girls ushered us into the "Tête-à-Tête", a side street café with miniature jukeboxes and cosy booths, good coffee and chocolate cake. The cooing waitress served Elvis first, but was hissed away by Betty who considered Elvis already her very own. Alice had me as the second prize. They liked our English clothes and accents, laughed at our sailor jokes and talked of saving their money for a trip to England. We saw a lot of Betty and Alice; they regularly arrived at the wharf and always knew our whereabouts wherever we were in Wellington.

Passenger ship departures were always festive occasions and *Rangitoto's* sailing day was no exception. The engine room throbbed with readiness. The passengers were settling aboard. The Blue Peter fluttered at the yardarm. The hatches were battened down. Tugs lurked at bow and stern, and crew shore leave ended at 1pm.

At 2pm I found myself with a group of Scottish shipmates engaged in a whisky drinking session with other ship's crews, newly arrived with no pressure to return to their vessels. The Third Mate burst into the bar just as the *Rangitoto* sounded urgent blasts on her booming whistle. His entrance had us all laughing with defiant drunkenness.

Shortly afterwards a squad of constables arrived to herd us outside and back to the ship with prodding batons. Alice and Betty were among the huge crowd to farewell family and friends with their coloured streamers. I lurched toward Alice for a goodbye kiss and was pounced upon by two large uniforms.

In the melée, a police helmet bounced at my feet as the crowd roared approval. I was quickly put to the ground, handcuffed then unceremoniously dragged up the last remaining gangway under the disapproving glares of the Captain and passengers.

I awoke the following morning with a severe headache and a request for my presence in the Captain's office. *Rangitoto* had left Wellington without my assistance. I was heavily fined for my absences and disgraceful behaviour. The New Zealand Shipping Company could do without the likes of me sullying its hard earned reputation. My services would be terminated on arrival in London.

Flash called me a legend and invited me to his local pub to assist his next punch up.

Colin became very morose on our return to Tahiti. His flood of letters had come to an end, so did his diving. Elvis and I swam without him. In Panama he received one solitary, unscented letter. It was a Dear John Letter. His sweetheart had become very impressed with the attention of his friend. They were to be married. She wanted Colin to be Best Man.

Berthed back in London we lined up in the crew mess room to sign off the ship's articles. Ginger Moxley was re-signing eager deckhands for the following trip and placing crews on other company vessels. I caught his eye over his battered briefcase, there was a solemn shaking of the carrot coloured head and a definite tut tut tutting sound. I knew if he spoke, it would be to tell me to sling my hook. My New Zealand Shipping Company experience was over.

Elvis went into partnership with a wealthy woman who owned a number of hairdressing salons in up market London. She also bought him a Jaguar sports car.

UNION-CASTLE LINE TO SOUTH AND EAST AFRICA

THE UNION-CASTLE ROYAL MAIL STEAMER "PRETORIA CASTLE" 28,625 TONS

Pretoria Castle

The Golden Voyage

Back on another liner, back to South Africa, back on watches, back on the lookout, back scrubbing decks, back in a four-berth cabin, back in the tropics and happy.

We dropped off bags of mail and stores at the Azores then called into Madeira for the passengers' first trip ashore.

On to Las Palmas in the Canary Islands, the same traders selling the same goods with the same eagerness as on my first visit there. This time I took it all in my stride and was sober when we departed.

South past Cape Verde Islands, crossing the Equator, again King Neptune pretending to be an obese, tattooed seaman has the passengers happy. Tropical birds watch from above.

The small British island of St. Helena was just a rock sticking out of the sea more than a thousand miles off the West African coast. It had been Napoleon's prison from 1815–1821. Then some Boer prisoners had enjoyed its solitude in 1900.

A long way south and just as remote was a small group of volcanic islands called Tristan Da Cunha. They had been evacuated by the British barely a year before. The families were re-settled in Cape Town and London.

Six of our deck hands were from the Islands. They were of a dusky complexion, cheerful hard workers and very good seamen. They were also very emotional and misty-eyed being so close to their home, hoping to return in the near future.

Heading directly east for Cape Town we ploughed and dipped through the famous mountainous Cape Rollers created by the merging of the Atlantic and Indian Oceans at the well-named Cape of Good Hope. Eventually we berthed safely under the massive Table Mountain.

I was back in this strange separated land with separate bars and hotels, separate seats in parks, separated buses and taxis. Separated everything.

Seeing signs stating 'Whites Only' or 'Blacks Only' stabbed at my soul, but they were rules that had to be obeyed.

Our watch was put in charge of cargo security in No.4 hold. It proved to be an impossible task.

Armed with a bunch of keys to open one cargo locker for access and to lock another to avoid pilfering at the same time was hopeless. Surrounded by a teeming local workforce who sang, sweated and laughed as they toiled had me feeling like a lone white policeman.

It was the same in Port Elizabeth, East London and Durban discharging our general cargo then reloading South African goods in the same ports for the return trip to England.

Then, one day there was great excitement aboard.

The ship's grapevine was abuzz with a story that aboard *Cape Town Castle* our sister ship, a large amount of gold bullion was missing. It had vanished on the high seas sometime during the passage between Cape Town and Southampton.

An ex-shipmate had signed on her as an AB. We had agreed to ship out together for South Africa while on the *Orcades* but a twist of fate saw us sign on different ships of the same company and I never saw him again.

Mischief should have been Frank's middle name. An Australian, with a healthy streak of non-conformity, there was a touch of Ned Kelly about Frank too. He was always pushing boundaries and had led me astray more than once during the *Orcades* voyage.

When the news of the missing gold came through I thought only of Frank. He was on that ship; he had the audacity to pull off such a stunt. I had a strong premonition that Frank would be involved. Once we were berthed back in Southampton, many more details about the brazen theft of the gold emerged.

A larger than usual amount of gold had been loaded aboard *Cape Town Castle*. With the ship's strong room full, a baggage room was used to store the excess crates of gold. The baggage room was double locked with large padlocks then sealed with the official government seal. The seals and locks were visually checked at the end of each watch during the trip to England.

When the Royal Mint Security Guards unloading the gold discovered the crime, the whole port of Southampton was closed down and bristled with police and SAS troops. The missing gold was headline news.

Even the captain and first-class passengers were searched at all gates while a massive rummage squad combed every nook and cranny on the liner for days on end unsuccessfully. Eventually it was time for the *Cape Town Castle* to return to sea with the gold still missing.

Frank and his pal had signed back on the ship for another voyage with all other regular crew. They were not suspected. A number of plainclothes policemen had also signed on as stewards while a smaller squad of customs men sailed with her to continue their search for the missing gold.

Just prior to the ship's departure from Southampton a seaman visited a back street passport photo shop with a false moustache, horn-rimmed glasses and an assumed name. The following morning the shop owner reported it to the police who contacted the liner at sea, then the shipboard sleuths grabbed their man.

The newspapers reported that two seamen appeared in court charged with stealing twenty bars of gold, worth £200,000, on the high seas. Police acting on a tip recovered the gold from hiding places on the ship after it returned to South Africa.

I followed the story with relish and headed for the nearest pub where the unreported facts were spilled with humour and wit by the well-oiled mariners who had been on the voyage.

The temporary strong room had an Achilles heel. Frank and another seaman had found it. Working through the nights the lads had climbed down a ventilator shaft supplying fresh air to the lower spaces from huge cowls on deck. A light grille was easily removed and the gold bars then transferred to a large empty sand bin. The gold was cemented into the bottom of the bin that was then filled with sand. The two seamen had planned to stay aboard the *Cape Town Castle* for another trip then remove the gold in South Africa at their leisure.

Being locked in a small cabin with four angry policemen was enough to have Frank's partner singing like a canary.

During the search for the gold, the red-faced customs men had twice prodded the sand in the ingenious hiding place with rods but had not thought to empty out the sand.

It was Frank with the false moustache.

Waipawa

Waipawa

She was not built for speed. My single cabin was basic and roomy. A leisurely leaving from Liverpool on a bright spring day was a pleasant change from the previous voyage on the *Corinthic* which was always in panic mode at mooring or departure times. Wooden decks the length of the ship were a sign of older days. She was easy to manage and never a chore with her simple steam winches and no heavy lifting gear, plus tarpaulins on the hatches.

Last in the Suez Canal convoy seemed her rightful place and our eventual arrival in Fremantle almost went unnoticed. *Waipawa* wallowed around the ports of Australia and finally across to New Zealand where we whiled away many days in many ports.

In the port of Napier I used my weekend to add the *Waipawa* name to the many other ships' names painted on the cliff face overlooking the port. A photo of my endeavours appeared in the local paper. I was an ant-sized speck on the end of a rope. In most New Zealand ports our crew was required to help with loading cargo.

One day while working with a gang of watersiders loading frozen sheep from a railway wagon, one of them addressed me with a sneer. "What did you get up to last night, Pom?" He had been working night shift on another ship and often did. Although I resented his manner, I readily recounted the events of a house party, happily painting him a picture of almost rampant debauchery.

There was a soft chuckling from the group as his questions took on a hard edge. I described the house and its location to the now hissing interrogator, adding that all rooms were packed with bodies. Rock and roll was blaring, beer flowing and that it seemed every seaman in port was there. Suddenly, he lurched from the wagon and ran from the wharf under a cloud of laughter. Evidently he was unaware of his wife's nocturnal activities with visiting sailors.

Before we sailed for home, a dance with a talent contest was held at the Flying Angel mission to Seamen. The dance was the usual formal affair with smiling matrons proffering plates of cakes and strong hot tea to sober sailors. A makeshift band on a stage consisted of a battered piano with yellow keys at which a local sheep-shearer with banana fingers and mad eyes thrashed out old favourites with the assistance of a callow lad with lank blond hair, pimples, and a small drum kit.

The padre's attractive teenage daughter was in hot demand by a long line of lecherous lads, but her only conversation was of our salvation and Jesus Christ. Some lamented the need for a good Catholic girl.

The talent contest began with a young steward giving a very passable version of an Elvis Presley ballad. A heavily pregnant friend of the Padre's wife sang a joyous hymn which was followed by a toothless ship's fireman playing the spoons. The padre's daughter sang something from an Italian opera to wild applause from the local ladies. It seemed she was hopefully destined for the Italian stage.

A German squeezed some terrible sounds from a worn button squeezebox, after that a bulbous Scot sang about lights in Aberdeen. Then it was my turn, the final act. As I stepped onto the stage, the manic pianist took a surreptitious swig from a hidden flask and gave me a knowing wink. As the beaming padre introduced me to the dwindling mob. I heard one of my shipmates groan not so sotto voce, "Oh no."

The pianist liked my choice of song - the Jim Reeves hit song 'He'll have to go'. Banana fingers started without me with the now lively youth banging loudly along in his wake. I was still asking her to put her lips closer to the phone as he galloped to the end leaving me groaning the last words. 'He'll have to go'. The drummer boy came to a reluctant, clumsy stop as I left the stage to nil applause. The child bearer was announced the winner, second was the padre's daughter and surprisingly, spoons came third. The last dance was held. The last limp sandwiches were grabbed. Then, as we all wandered back to our vessels with midnight looming, the only comment on my talent was "You murdered that song."

One Sunday afternoon on the long, slow, homeward voyage across the Pacific, I lay on my bunk with the swishing sound of the sea and the soft ship's heartbeat below the only sounds. It was as though I was alone on a deserted ship. I left my body. A strange, surreal experience, I was floating above my body looking down on myself lying on the bunk. I was swathed in a bright white light but my body was as a negative photograph. It was a pleasurable feeling with an inner peace for many days afterwards. It never happened again.

Slowly through the wonder of the Panama Canal and back to a chilly Liverpool the voyage had taken exactly eight months to complete. All other ships in the fleet did the same trip in five months.

On the London bound train drinking and singing was on the menu.

'He'll have to go' was sung more than once.

Satisfying my need for speed. Triumph 110

Shipboard Harmony

In 1967 with manpower shortages and declining discipline, the British Merchant Navy bigwigs decided something had to be done to stop the rot. A scheme was devised to send all petty officers and those with potential to a weeklong supervisors' course run by a retired sea captain.

The venue was a small hotel in the seaside town of Brighton, England, with its own pub on the ground floor. Although I had blotted my copybook on a number of occasions while under the "affluence of incohol", I was marked as one with potential and chosen to attend course No.3.

On the first evening after booking in, I traced the sounds of raucous laughter to the bar and discovered most of the class of twenty already settled in and swapping yarns. This latest burst of laughter was about the young chambermaid who was left blushing by a note pinned to a door, which read: SHAKE SOFTLY HALFWAY DOWN-- IF HARD KEEP SHAKING. It was seamen's humour to the fore and an excellent start.

Over the next few days the Captain with a team of cheerful experts would teach us the art of public speaking and positive leadership skills. We would also study the history of the Seamen's Union, industrial relations, the Merchant Shipping Act plus many different ways to motivate the numerous recalcitrant personnel that infested the British Merchant Fleet in these Swinging Sixties.

One visiting speaker lecturing on "Setting a Good Example" removed his gold wristwatch at the beginning of the session and placed it on the desk to keep one eyeball on the time. Much of his time was spent under a cloud of chalk dust as he wrote statistics and key phrases on a blackboard. He then waited for us to make notes before erasing them under yet another cloud of chalk dust. At the end of the session, the watch had disappeared and was never seen again.

In the bar after evening lectures, pupils and tutors mixed with an egalitarianism that was both refreshing and delicate.

We used each others' Christian names with a degree of uncomfortable caution. It wasn't the "Fair Dinkum" Australasian model, where Jack was as good as his master, as long as he did his job. Our British class system was well ingrained.

On the last night our tutors were treated to a unique session of smutty nautical humour in recognition of their hard work and patience.

We, the seasoned seafaring comedians working as a team, held them and the locals in the palms of our hands with rapid fire blue jokes while the barman was kept busy serving the rum and, as usual, the tone was lowered as the evening wore on.

It was said: the chambermaid was so innocent, she thought wanking was somewhere in China and with a packet of wine gums, a swing around a lamppost she would be well pissed and want to know any seaman named Dick. The Golden Rivet and Porthole jokes got polished until there were no apples for young Jim Boy to grab from the barrel. All the penis jokes got an airing, starting with someone describing how he'd made his penis six inches long by folding it in half. This was outdone by someone claiming he'd achieved a ten-inch member by cutting two inches off the end. Another had twelve inches but didn't use it as a rule and yet another sailor had one leg shorter than the other two. The laughter was non-stop and the rum flowed freely.

Then an Irishman recited the famous "Farting Competition":

There will be a Grand Farting Competition at the Arse Hall.

Trousers must be down by 7.30 pm.

Competitors will either fart or be disqualified.

One point would be awarded for a Freep.

Five points would be awarded for a Flutterblast.

Ten points would be awarded for a Double-Flutterblast.

The Main Contest would be between Lord Windowsmear of England and Paul Boomer of Australia, both long time rivals and living on a diet of cabbage.

Windowsmear, arrogant in gusset-less purple silk tights and cravat, starts with a conservative Freep without gripping the Farting Post.

Boomer bounces on stage and brazenly lets off a Flutterblast.

Then says, "Pick the bones out of that you Pommie Prick."

Windowsmear complains about Boomer's stench to no avail.

Boomer and Windowsmear both gripping the Farting post, trade fart for fart.

It all finally ends with Windowsmear doing a terrible follow-through Splashfart which clears the Hall. Windowsmear is disqualified. Boomer wins.

It was a most enjoyable session until there was the ugly sight of a well-oiled cook from the Cornish port of Falmouth who'd become bellicose and foulmouthed. He loudly accused the bemused barman of "shortchanging". The laughter came to an abrupt halt.

Removing the reluctant cook from the bar under the watchful eyes of our tut-tutting mentors was an exercise in restraint. Showing that the lectures on leadership and harmony had not gone to waste, the drunken cook was gently coaxed from the bar by three composed colleagues until out of earshot. Then the nautical solution was applied.

Later, a man with a bloody nose was seen boarding the late evening train to Cornwall while the rest of us future leaders from around Britain were awarded a "Certificate of Attendance" and returned to our ships with the assumption that we were now better leaders of men.

Afric

A Speedy Trip

I signed on the MV*Afric* on 6 December 1963 outward bound for Australia, tropical weather and a four-month voyage. It was perfect timing to avoid another British winter. If the *Waipawa* was a slow sea-slug, the *Afric* was a fast flying-fish with a cruising speed of 16 knots and more. German-built with racy lines, she had recently beaten a Dutch ship's record on the unofficial wool race from New Zealand. Light ship, we scudded across the North Sea winter waves to load a general cargo in Hamburg and Bremen.

It was the skipper's first command after serving many years as mate and relieving skipper. He was very proud of his ocean greyhound. In a thick fog we sought the anchorage at the mouth of the river Elbe. The carpenter and I stood ready to drop the anchor. The deck-boy rang the bell.

Ships' sirens and bells rang in the white blanket all around us as the skipper zigzagged through the crowded anchorage perilously close to ghostly shapes of ships at a seemingly fast clip while snapping orders from the radar screen on the bridge. Suddenly, there was yelling from the wheelhouse, our siren was in panic mode, our engine racing full astern. The empty ship shuddered and shook in protest as the propeller churned the green sea into foam.

Dead ahead of us a white shape emerged. It was a fully laden oil tanker already safely anchored. A voice yelled "Hang on" just as our bow hit the tanker in her stern crew quarters. There was a brief, eerie silence before the pandemonium of klaxons, sirens, bells and human shouts filled the wet, white surroundings with a confused cacophony. Looking over the bow we saw a crewman in blue-striped pyjamas staring up at us from his wrecked cabin, a look of disbelief frozen on his face. Our prepared anchor hung above him for what seemed an eternity until we finally pulled astern. I was reminded of the first piece removed from a birthday cake.

Riding high in the water, our bow was undamaged and we eventually anchored, feeling very lucky to have missed her oil tanks. A flurry of radio messages between the ship and Head Office had the strutting new captain more like a worried mouse with a lot of explaining to do. Two days later the fog had lifted and a gruff overweight river pilot with leather boots and overcoat climbed aboard to take us up the busy river Elbe to Hamburg.

This time, I was the helmsman taking orders in sharp German/English when the fog closed in again and shrouded us in an ice cold white blanket just as we rounded a bend at half-speed. Eight knots was full speed for the ancient *Waipawa* so it seemed that everything aboard the *Afric* was done at full pace. The nervous skipper looked like a startled ferret as he constantly scurried from the radar screen to the bridge wings. My fingers gripped the wheel with excited anticipation as all my instincts warned me of danger ahead.

Suddenly, the pilot snatched the megaphone and began screaming a string of throaty guttural words into the fog ahead while at the same time blowing our impressive foghorn. Two returning trawlers ahead of us were treated to the German alphabet, back to front, inside out and upside down. In no time at all, they were close on our starboard bow, restricting our movements and very soon we were on top of them. By now the hairs on my neck were twitching as the terrible guttural instructions increased in volume and rapidity. There was a healthy panic in the air as a foreign foghorn sounded close-by. The pilot and skipper began elbowing each other around the radar screen. Briefly, it seemed I was watching a Laurel and Hardy comedy.

The skipper started to wave his arms as if trying to fly away. It was instantly obvious that he'd lost his nerve and relinquished all control to the beefy pilot. Openly hostile, the red-faced pilot was hissing horrible, spittle-laden German words into the skipper's ashen face as a large ship came out of the fog. It was painted white. The impact was a deafening boom, followed by a long screeching of tortured steel as both ships ground against each other until finally breaking free and disappearing back into the fog. We were back on an even keel and still moving up river apace. The wheelhouse was bedlam. The skipper was crying openly and the pilot continued to scream foul words at him.

We went straight to the repair yards with a thirty-foot gash in our portside and with the other ship's anchor still embedded in our side like a fly stuck on flypaper. Our gangway was turned into match-wood while the whole port side looked like a scrap yard. Our port lifeboat was left aboard the other ship.

The other ship's anchor stuck to our side

Parts of the other ship's bow in the chief steward's bunk

The next day I was required at the Court of Enquiry in a plush maritime lawyers' office taking an oath on a German bible. I gave my account of events in front of a collection of legal eagles, both company agents and the pilot's very own mouthpiece. The ship's logbooks were intently scrutinised as a pretty young fraulein served me first with bagels and coffee. I felt very important indeed.

The skipper appeared a broken man. Two collisions in three days on his first command was not a good start. The next day we were signed-off in a dry dock and sent back to England for an unscheduled Christmas at home just nine days after we were hired.

A Trip with the Beatles

The *Afric* was repaired and ready for sea again within a month and I re-joined her back in Hamburg with a new captain and crew loading for New Zealand. The Beatles had taken over the pop world and the younger lads aboard had Beatle hairstyles and clothes. Winklepicker shoes, bumfreezer jackets, narrow ties and high collared shirts were the latest fashion.

Four of them always went ashore looking like the famous Fab Four creating a stir wherever they went. The locals waved and greeted them like real celebrities and they soaked it up with good humour. At sea they were hard working lads in paint-spattered dungarees. But going ashore they were a sight for sore eyes.

Back in summertime Wellington the hot news was the Beatles were heading for New Zealand. This was grist for the mill for our Beatle Boys. They trotted down the gangway on arrival day shrouded by a heavy waft of Old Spice aftershave, although none was a shaver.

The crowded wharf was brought to a standstill as everyone, ashore and aboard watched the well-tailored lads tiptoe their winklepickers through the maze of trucks, crates and bales. As they passed a group of stevedores, one of them loudly asked the most angelic lad if he would like to become a Beatle. Stopping in his tracks, the cherubic face smiled brilliantly and replied: "Yeah. Yeah. Yeah."

"Come here and I'll make yer Ringo," said the stevedore. The ship and wharf erupted with laughter as the lad, blushing red and bristling, hurried through the gates with his pals to the nearest coffee bar with a jukebox.

Ashore, they were in constant demand by the young ladies of Wellington. One was a very attractive wayward daughter of the vulgar stevedore.

There were many comical characters on the Kiwi wharves. One of them was a bearded and humorous stevedore nicknamed "Spud" who subtly turned my greeting into a discussion on the merits of a good British kipper within seconds. They were well sought after and as good as cash. Nudge. Nudge. Wink. Wink. It was a year since he'd tasted a good kipper. He preferred the Scottish kippers to the Tyneside. Very soon a dozen kippers from the obliging cook put a sparkle in Spud's eye and we became instant friends. Spud took me home to meet his family one weekend. We took a train to a place called Upper Hutt and everyone aboard greeted Spud. On arrival we climbed into a 1930s Model-A Tudor saloon car then rattled our way on a gravel road to a place called Te Marua.

There was a rifle under canvas on the backseat; Spud asked me to hand it to him as we came to a stop. The bolt and bullets came out of thin air and were quickly clicked into place.

"See that hare over there?" Hare? What hare? Where?

I had good eyesight and feverishly searched the dry, brown hillside to no avail as the barrel of the rifle came past my nose and poked through the open window. Spud squinted down the sights and squeezed the trigger. The blast in my ears had a positive effect on my eyesight. It was then I saw the hare as it tumbled down the hill towards the road.

It was expertly gutted and skinned, then bagged and soon we were trundling along the dusty road again to his cabin in the hills.

Spud's cheerful wife Rae welcomed us at the door with their two young giggling daughters. The interior was rustic log cabin, with an impressive rack of hunting rifles with telescopic sights. As President of the Deerstalkers Association, Spud was an avid hunter, known in every hotel, a member of the local Lodges and a dental technician in his spare time.

Trophy stag horns, heads of chamois and thar were mounted on the walls. The polished wooden floors were scattered with deer pelts. All bagged by Spud himself and all with a story attached. Spud was a hearty and generous host.

Michelle and Joann tittered as they set the huge rough-sawn table while Rae produced a fabulous roast of venison with all the trimmings.

Just before bedtime we walked a short distance from the house. Spud cupped his hands to his mouth and let out a strange, long roar into the night. Within seconds a stag answered his roar from a nearby ridge and my hair stood on end. This Brixton boy was a long way from home and loving it. Spud tugged his beard with a satisfied grin.

As dawn broke we were armed and climbing a steep hill, talking in whispers, inspecting tracks and spoors. Some were fresh. I was directed with urgent mime to climb the other side of a steep damp cliff. Using my feet, knees, elbows, hands, fingernails and, one time, even my chin, I noisily clambered upward.

Nearing the crest and puffing loudly, I stopped to look skyward and gazed straight into the eyeball of a stag, calmly staring down at me. With my feet firmly lodged, I fumbled my rifle from my back and took aim, but like magic it had disappeared and I was left wondering if my imagination had been playing tricks on me.

Later, Spud pointed to the tracks of the stag and its four hinds. It had been observing me long before I had spotted it. I was lucky I hadn't shot it. It could have fallen on top of me sending me plummeting to my death.

I was fish out of water again.

The next morning we collected mushrooms with the girls, taking them home for Rae to add to the breakfast.

That same weekend there was much excitement among friends and neighbours with a barbeque fired up to celebrate the installation of the "Flushy". The long drop at the bottom of the garden was a thing of the past and the Tatham family's social status was now much improved.

On sailing day they arrived in their Model A to wave goodbye and make it a memorable New Zealand moment.

We scooted around the coast loading bales of wool, tins of lambs' tongues, corned beef, sheep and cow-skins, and drums of tallow in the picturesque ports of Timaru, Port Chalmers and Lyttleton.

We powered across the Pacific, zipped through the Panama Canal, and scooted across the Atlantic on a fast clip homeward. Scuttlebutt on the company grapevine was that the original skipper, demoted back to mate, had run amok in his cabin with a fire axe.

He was taken ashore in a padded jacket with leather straps.

Iberic

A Liverpool Trip

At 25 years of age I agreed to take over the bosun's job on the *Iberic* while the regular bosun and crew took their shore leave. I was sent to Liverpool.

Luckily I had an older bunch of sailors to work with, most of whom only did home trade trips, relieving jobs and deliveries to repair yards. One old-timer had been at sea before I was born and had survived a torpedo on an Atlantic Convoy during the war.

Two others were ex-bosuns. The first was unwilling to take the pressures of the job with the new attitude of "let it all hang out and challenge everything" that was sweeping Britain and the Merchant Navy. The second was an Irishman in his forties who had a constant battle with the bottle who regularly and loudly advised me on many issues.

Generally, I was pleased to have their collective experience. Until the night the boozer staggered up the gangway and wobbled to a stop at the top. Then, with a stage entrance that a professional actor would have been proud of, he took a baleful look at me and slurred: "I was in Baghdad before you were in your Dad's bag; lad." He disappeared below decks, heading for his bunk.

The next morning, I challenged his behaviour, even though he was old enough to be my father. Generously apologetic, he helped himself to one of my smokes and said that the devil had taken him last night. He frequently used that statement while under the influence. It was one of his many party pieces. It was also blarney at its best.

Liverpool, always a good run ashore, lived up to its reputation once again with a visit to the famous dockside pub known as Mabel's. A popular rough and ready place, it was a favourite watering hole for seamen and dockers alike.

One night I found myself in a cosy corner with two local sisters with the harshest Liverpool accents imaginable. The eldest was an attractive 26-year-old with a well-acquainted Irishman in tow. Her younger dolly-bird sister was about 19 years old, blue eyed and blonde. We kept them entertained with endless patter, many compliments and gin and tonics till closing time.

Arm in arm, we walked the short distance to their humble terraced house with two painted concrete steps and no hallway. The lovers grabbed the only settee. Dolly sat on my lap in an armchair as we watched the groping passionate players.

Earlier, I had noticed a light under the kitchen door plus the sound of dishes being washed. I assumed it was Mother.

The ardent lovers headed for the bedroom, the Irishman gave me a knowing wink while Dolly's sister gave a thumbs-up sign. Then we were alone.

Manfully, I took Dolly's hand over to the still warm settee and gazed lustfully into her pretty blue eyes – just like they did in the movies. Unsure if I was looking at a startled rabbit or a beautiful experienced young woman like her sister I eased her back onto the settee and discreetly released my passion.

As she touched the liberated phallus she let out a piercing scream and dug her fingernails into my face and raked my cheek, leaving me instantly flaccid and bleeding.

Suddenly there was mayhem. A fierce looking woman with hair curlers and a raised rolling pin flung the kitchen door open and rushed at me. My dash for the front door was pure instinct, but my frantic fumbling with the lock for a quick exit was comic. The dragon rounded the settee at speed and managed to trap my foot in the door.

There was an eerie moment when the only sound was her wheezing anger mixed with a smell of disinfectant. After what seemed like an eternity, I was sprinting freely on the road with the screeching harridan well astern. As the rolling pin whistled past my ear I let out a relieved cackle, running non-stop to the safety of the docks with the rescued rolling pin as a souvenir.

The following morning the crew approval for the disfigured young bosun was overt. Back in Mabel's the next night Dolly had the nerve to ask me for a drink. I bought her one but declined the offer to take her home.

Three weeks later the regular boatswain rejoined in Rotterdam and I returned to London. My first trip as boatswain was a success.

Afric

Snapped on Schnapps

The *Arabic* was a sister ship to the *Afric* so I was acquainted with her rigging and layout. I relieved her bosun in the port of Hull on a cold, wet November day in 1964 for the home trade run and quickly established a good rapport with the leathery-faced Geordie carpenter.

Two of the deck-hands had stayed on from the previous voyage – one a beefy lad from Liverpool; the other, a wiry, unruly, Yorkshireman with a broken nose and trouble in his eyes. All three were good mates – they laughed and drank a lot. Things ran very smoothly with them aboard, but ashore it was a different story.

This was Yorky's hometown; his playground, and he knew every barmaid in every pub in Hull. One night we found ourselves in a popular pub called the Paragon with a group of trawlermen's wives, celebrating their men's recent sailing. The jukebox thumped Elvis and Beatle songs while the tipsy women danced with any willing male until closing time.

Yorky didn't return to the ship with us; he'd slipped away earlier with one of the fishwives. But they, and everyone else, were blissfully unaware that the fishing fleet was forced back to port in the early hours by North Sea gales.

One suspicious trawlerman furtively arrived home at 3am, tattooed loudly on his own front door with the hilt of his gutting knife, then crept silently around the house to the back door.

Yorky's description of his exit was both hilarious and riveting. In his underpants, carrying his shoes and clothes, he'd jumped into the arms of the furious fisherman. The outcome was obviously one-sided, as his bruised face told of his escape through hedges and back gardens with a stab wound in his right buttock and without most of his clothes.

Two days later, Yorky was happy to be back aboard, battling storms and heading for Germany, while back in Hull a fisherman cursed and honed his knife.

We moored at a small riverside berth outside Bremen for routine engine maintenance on a foggy afternoon.

A small bar a short distance away was the only attraction in the bleak surroundings and soon we were sampling schnapps around the tables with the smiling host in poised attendance with an icy bottle.

He encouraged us to knock on the table each time we shot the schnapps into our throats, thus signalling for a refill. Naturally, this brought much laughter with constant knocking and by the time evening arrived we were all "Brahms and Liszt", pissed.

The bar soon filled. The local frauleins arrived from their offices, hotly followed by the local lads eager to investigate the invading Englanders at their watering hole. The jukebox played, the joint jumped, bodies bumped and the room spun. With a chubby fraulein in my arms I danced an imitation of Elvis Presley with a windmill arm and thrusting pelvis, while acknowledging the applauding drunken crew.

A sneering local youth purposely bumped into me each time we met on the tiny dance square, interfering with my equilibrium. I informed Scouse of my dilemma, saying that if it happened again I would give the sneering Kraut a bunch of fives.

It did happen again and I hit him.

Blood spattered the dress of his fraulein, who screamed strange angry words at me as my chubby partner disappeared and the concerned host cut off the jukebox. In the brooding silence that followed, the Germans and British separated, oozing mutual malice in the tinderbox atmosphere as sirens sounded in the distance.

I was being both protected and punched in a melée when armed, green-leathered police burst in and took control.

The young lad had not been sneering at me. His face was the result of a shipyard accident, which had left him scarred with a hare lip. He was the town's favourite son.

The bar was closed. We were ordered back to the ship, running a gauntlet of abuse all the way to the gangway and beyond. Future shore leave was "Verboten" for the remaining days of our stay. Scouse later informed me that I had been bumping into everyone else.

I've treated schnapps with caution ever since.

A night on the schnapps. From L., Yorky, Chippie, Scouse, author.

The Black Cat

As we arrived in Genoa early one morning a disappointed groan was heard from the crew because the American 7th fleet was in port. US Navy ships occupied all the best berths nearest the best bars.

It meant the price of drinks would be inflated; the bars crowded; taxis available to only US Navy uniforms and the bar girls would be overworked. But most importantly, the risk of a social disease increased.

Genoa was a popular port so after a long hot day we headed ashore to quench our thirst. The streets were a teeming mass of people, honking cars and taxis. American Military Police with batons strutted among the swaggering sailors keeping the peace. Others in jeeps scowled as they prowled.

All of the bars were overflowing onto the streets and needed determined pushing just to reach the bar with our meagre amounts of spending money. As the night wore on, our crew wandered back to the ship in disgruntled groups.

But for me the night was young. I was on a Hollywood movie set. The music and lights, the throng, tumult and clamour attracted me like a moth to a flame, fuelled by cheap Italian wine.

I found the "Black Cat" in a back alley in the early hours and my luck changed. Here, away from the main streets, the girls were older, broader and a little past their prime but there was room to move. I lurched to the bar and found a large stentorian American named Bob perched on a barstool.

His ample buttocks hung like loosely furled sails, his belly rested in his lap and his splayed flabby arms took up more than his fair share of the bar top. A semi-circle of drinks, coins, cigarettes, Zippo lighter and a small pile of Yankee dollars kept a Fading Beauty close to his side.

After a few drinks and a visit to the pungent urinal I returned to find my space at the bar much reduced and Bob's sizeable bulk leaning heavily to starboard. With a vigorous elbow and imitating his American twang, I said loudly: "Move over, Blob."

I ducked the expected back hander. Fortunately, he was still firmly glued to the stool and I was still on my feet. I booted the stool from under him. His chin hit the bar rail and he hit the floor with a thump with me straddling and punching him. Suddenly, the whole bar was yelling and cheering me. Or so I thought. The barstool had crashed into the Signora's shins and had drawn blood. It was her operatic lungs that were responsible for the dramatic noise.

Until that moment I felt I was giving a reasonable account of myself with the fat Navy man until I saw a burst of stars and fell to my knees. The angry Signora had fitted the barstool across the back of my head and now Blob had me helpless in a headlock and was pummelling my face with a fist festooned with flashy rings.

I awoke bloodied in the back seat of a police car heading for I knew not where, as the first fingers of dawn crept into the sky.

I was driven into a courtyard, babbling and then deserted by the two young, posing policemen wearing high leather boots, who needed an interpreter. The car windows were instantly filled with faces of urchins, also babbling, who scattered and yelled pandemonium as I leapt from the car and ran down a cobblestone alley with my sailor's homing device locked on automatic pilot.

I sprinted downhill, turning left and right and left again with the sounds of the yelling urchins fading and the sounds of police sirens now out there hunting for me. Darting from cover to cover like a hunted fox, I finally reached the docks, but was dismayed to see my ship across the dock, a long way away.

I struck lucky. I spotted a long line of unattended gondolas moored side-by-side awaiting their day. Without hesitation, I clambered across them as though they were stepping-stones, waking a furious night watchman in my stride.

With the watchman waving at the sky and the sirens wailing, I freed the offside gondola with a healthy shove which sent it out into the dock. With thumping heart and only one oar, I sculled across to the cheering crew, enjoying the commotion across the water at the start of their day. As the police cars drove around the dock road toward us, I scrambled up the rope ladder and quickly disappeared below decks to safety.

The chase was over; the sirens went silent and returned to base.

The gondola was recovered and I remained aboard for the rest of our stay in Genoa.

Safely back aboard!

Persic

A Trip to Paradise

From an upper deck the mate and I watched the lively, longhaired crew arrive with their bags, radios and guitars.

It was 1966 and, like the Beatles and Rolling Stones, everybody was sporting long hair and our new crew was no exception. It was obvious some of them were already well acquainted from previous voyages. The mate's remark that they seemed to think they're going on a cruise was the first inkling of future trouble and of things to come.

The start of the voyage was positive and exciting. Everyone from the skipper to the galley-boy was fizzing with the knowledge of our itinerary. We were on our way to New Zealand via the South Pacific paradise of Rarotonga in the Cook Islands and to Fiji as a bonus.

For most British seamen it was a rare opportunity to experience this exotic, fabled island that was off the normal shipping routes. Visiting Rarotonga was a dream come true.

The deck-hands were a happy, hard-working bunch. Any bosun would be pleased to have such an eager crew. The young skipper was emigrating to take a company job in

Wellington and was to be relieved there. The last thing he needed was trouble on his final voyage.

Our first port of call was Curaçao, off the coast of Venezuela, basically a large oil refinery on a small island used for trans-shipping Venezuelan oil. It was also a bunkering port for cargo ships and fortunately a night ashore for our crew.

The clever Dutch had provided a wonderful play area for their tanker crews while in port. It was known as "Happy Valley" and a fleet of speeding taxis ferried us there. Venezuelan girls, brought over from the mainland, were housed in their own cabins in a huge wired compound with a guard on the gate.

They greeted us eagerly in the open sided bar and soon we were visiting their cabins. Someone said it was a haven for sailors. Medically checked and regularly replaced, most were slim and feisty with an uncanny knowledge of the world's coinage. "Happy Valley" nights were re-lived on the poopdeck at sunsets, as the Panama Canal came and went.

A lad known as "Walter Mitty" claimed he'd stolen back his payment from under the pillow while his hostess was in rapture at his sexual prowess. It was a story regularly told after a night ashore, and always brought a laugh, if told well.

Far from an ocean greyhound, the *Persic* lolled and rolled its way across the Pacific, trailing an endless ribbon of black smoke. On Saturday nights, movies were shown on a large canvas screen hoisted on the main mast under a swinging canopy of stars. Burning oily smuts from the funnel peppered the cast of cowboys as they rode the badlands of Texas and blotted the kiss between the handsome new marshall and the beautiful, recently widowed, owner of the town's only saloon.

Delayed by a tropical storm, we finally reached Rarotonga and cautiously approached the anchorage on a Sunday morning under a brooding, dark grey sky. The ship dragged its anchor with the stern pointing toward the reef a mere half a mile away, instead of the safer "parallel" position.

It was then that the nervous skipper made a very unpopular decision.

Over the ship's speaker system his message stated that because of the unsafe anchorage there would be no shore leave. There was great disappointment after the weeks of expectation.

The deck-hands were openly hostile and muttering of mutiny, while young dusky maidens wearing brightly coloured sarongs and blossoms in their hair, waved encouragement from the nearby shore. By now, the crew had made a decision; to swim ashore, defying the skipper's orders.

The third mate arrived at my elbow with an urgent request to join the skipper on the bridge. I found him with binoculars trying to identify a line of heads in the surf that were swimming for the shore.

Two of them had knives clamped in their teeth, presumably to fight off any monsters that may hinder their progress. One by one the skipper called their names while the second mate jotted them down on a pad. Then suddenly he made another decision. "If the sharks can't stop them, what chance do I have? Keep sea watches Mister Mate, and prepare both lifeboats for shore leave at noon."

On the stroke of noon the lifeboats were lowered in a tropical downpour. The second mate and engineer officers commandeered the motorboat while the rest of the deck crew, stewards and firemen were towed through the swell with the mate at the helm. It was like a scene from *Mutiny on the Bounty*.

Unfortunately, the motorboat towing us spluttered to a stop in the rain-drenched surf. The sight of a lifeboat being rowed by a group of ships' engineers was very comical. We rowed past laughing, to beat them ashore. The hare and the tortoise fable personified.

Meanwhile ashore, the original swimmers saw the boats coming and took to the hills, assuming we were coming to round them up.

Once ashore I wandered with the mate along a gravel road among the lush wet foliage and secretly wished I was with the lads. We walked into the cool Rarotongan Hotel, the largest building on the island, and the hub of all business.

Drinking chilled orange juice under a ceiling fan was a small group of white-haired European men and women. We accepted an invitation to join them and were served by a buxom Polynesian lady wearing a spotless white apron and a huge smile.

The mate was soon in deep discussions about the shipping trade, hurricane weather patterns and historical trivia, while I inwardly fidgeted and imagined the fun and mischief the rest of the crew were up to outside. Surely there was more to this Paradise Island than this group of geriatric colonials?

Through the open top walls of the ablution block I heard the tinkling sounds of female laughter and my spirits soared. I followed the laughter to the hotel laundry and to a sight that I would never forget.

Four beautiful, bare-breasted maidens worked around a large table pressing and folding crisp white bed sheets. The youngest, still in her early teens, giggled and quickly covered the most exquisite breasts I'd ever seen, while the older ones calmly covered themselves as I introduced myself and settled lustfully on the corner of the table. Bantering with the smiling girls, my reverie was interrupted by the arrival of the stern-faced hotel manager insisting on my immediate departure from the hotel. There was a stag-like attitude to his request.

Outside, some crew buzzed around on hired mopeds while others had found a house with a potent home brew. Evening fell, and now minus the mate, I found myself back among the laundry girls enjoying the setting sun. Embraced under a palm tree, I was in Paradise.

Two days later the original swimmers returned with their stories and the ship's routine was restored in time for the trip to Fiji and New Zealand.

The carefree skipper chose not to discipline the deserters, who now considered themselves heroes and responsible for the bubbling happiness aboard. He was relieved in Wellington by a grumpy, older skipper nearing retirement who believed in running a tight ship. But it was too late. The lads were out of control. The more he fined them the more they rebelled.

We left Wellington with three men in police custody, another two were left in an Auckland jail. Sailing around the NZ coast short-handed was no fun. In the port of Bluff, the drunken crew were still in the pub at sailing time, ignoring the impatient blasts of the ship's whistle.

The young third mate was dispatched to order the crew back aboard. He manfully strode into the bar, declining all offers of drink and relayed the captain's order in a quivering, high-pitched voice then hurried red-faced from the bar minus his uniform cap.

The barmaid commandeered the cap as the ship's cook firmly assured everyone that no British ship could put to sea without a cook aboard. So, more drinks were ordered.

The tide and itinerary was of more concern to our determined new skipper and with a final blast of the whistle we released the last mooring rope and left the troublesome crew behind.

I was happy to accept assistance from the chief steward, who also held a very important Chief Cook's certificate. The police, aided by the local rugby club, rounded up and jailed the drunken crew. Two days later in the port of Nelson they emerged from prison vans like returning war heroes.

The *Truth* newspaper, well known for blaring headlines, spicy stories, horseracing, and massage parlour advertisements, sent a reporter to interview the belligerent crew. A photo of the cheering lads filled the front page with screaming headlines. "Seamen Slam the Cops." Gestapo tactics, brutality and torture were used in the crew's version of events although they were all well groomed for the photo and minus any sign of ill treatment.

115

Finally ready for the homeward trip, the NZ police delivered the last of our missing crewmembers and watched with unfriendly eyes as we sailed away.

The dreary return voyage back to Liverpool with an unwilling, malevolent crew was indeed a long one.

Bleak winter weather seemed a fitting return to Liverpool.

Everyone from the skipper to the galley-boy was glad when the trip to Paradise was finally over.

With my souvenir sarong.

Jock's Last Trip

Angus McNeil was a comical twenty-two-year-old, and the only Scottish deck-hand among the London crew. He was an excellent seaman from a small Scottish island who declared he was born in a rowboat.

Everyone knew him as Jock and he had an uncanny knack of finding trouble whenever he went ashore. Although he loved a drink, he was also a slow paying tightwad in any drinking school and rarely carried his "sporran".

One night in Sydney, Jock and I headed down the gangway for a night ashore with a spring in our steps. Monty's, the first pub, was always worth checking out, so naturally we popped in for a quick one.

The main bar was speckled with some of our crew and a few locals, two of whom were men dressed as women and who coquettishly flicked their false eyelashes at us. Jock ensured that I bought the first beers. The beefy barman's lowered tones cautioned unnecessarily. "They're blokes."

But Jock without hesitation accepted an offer from the pink cashmere cardigan to buy him a drink. Unashamedly he ordered a double whisky with a beer chaser and decided to stay with his newfound benefactors.

I left Jock happily wedged between the attentive "ladies" at a corner table and went on my merry way. Although both our evenings were to be separate, they would both be very eventful.

My sojourn was a pub-crawl well away from the docks until the late hours found me both drunk and broke. With the sailor's inbuilt homing device, I staggered the strange dark streets heading for the docks, gripping a red oil lamp commandeered from a road works.

Finally, outside the dock gates I stopped to discreetly ease my bursting bladder against a high stone wall when I heard a vehicle come to a stop behind me. The unmistakable drawl of an Australian Constable asked loudly, "Where the fuck did yer get that?"

Still watering the wall, I called back over my shoulder. "I've had it all my life, mate." My London humour was not appreciated as the bulging blue uniform swung open the back door of the paddy wagon and said, "Get in, smart-arse."

Although happily drunk and just a short distance from the ship, any thoughts of running were out of the question. Barely able to walk and mesmerised by two flashlights, I meekly climbed in.

With three other drunks, I was bundled from the paddy wagon into a police station and ordered to empty my pockets onto a portly sergeant's desk. Once sober, I could be released after two hours with a payment of 30 shillings to find my own way back to the ship.

Unfortunately, my only possessions were 4 shillings and sixpence, five cigars, a box of matches, a cabin key and a belligerent attitude. Refusing to share my cigars and giving my name as "John Wayne" was not helpful, because very quickly I was shirt-fronted and renamed "Pommie Prick" through a blast of angry halitosis.

The large cell was almost full with about thirty snoring bodies on wooden pallets, some of whom were obviously wrestling with inner demons. I stood a while, muttering about my dilemma. I could not accept that I deserved to be among this specimen collection of Sydney finest gentlemen. Eventually I found a pallet and blanket near the toilet pan and slept soundly.

In the morning, dishevelled, coughing and spluttering, we were all driven a short distance and herded into a courtroom to await our sentences.

Sporting a carrot-coloured crew-cut a young judge arrived in a flurry, still fitting his wide lapelled brown jacket over his green shirt and bright yellow tie. Sprinting to his raised ornate chair he said g'day to Harry, Dave, Bruce and Bob as he tugged on his elastic tie. "Righto who's first?"

I followed a Norwegian seaman who blubbered in halting English something about his neighbour paying his wife too much attention in his absence. "Put a sock in it mate, you were here last week, fined £5. Next."

I admitted being drunk and carrying the red light for my own safety and was pleased there was no mention of indecent exposure. "Yer first time mate, next time I'll do yer, on yer bike." He was a refreshing change from the bleak-looking, black robed Brixton magistrate who put me away years before.

Safely back aboard ship I found that Jock had been severely beaten in an alley at closing time by the two frustrated female impersonators. Then on the homeward voyage he received a telegram from a Scottish lassie with news that he had successfully impregnated her on his last shore leave. She demanded marriage on his return home and Jock readily agreed with a return cable. That evening, we celebrated Jock's good fortune on the poopdeck. She was the only child of a wealthy couple who lived in a small castle on a large Scottish estate. A first class rail ticket to Glasgow Central Station awaited Jock on arrival back in London.

The last time I saw Jock he was swaggering down the gangway with a shouldered kitbag and whistling.

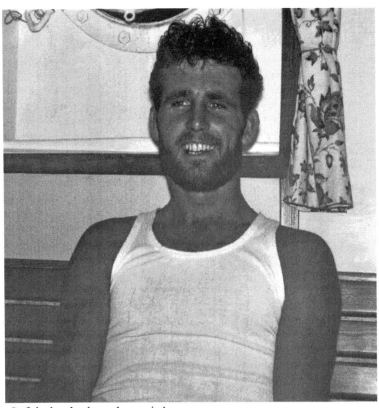

Safely back aboard...again!

The Storm Birds

I was on a ship once. It was a 70,000 tonne oil tanker sailing light ship from Cape Town. Heading north up the east coast of Africa we ran into stormy weather. Inside the Madagascar Channel the wind and seas funnelled to extreme, buffeting us relentlessly and making the lookout's job very uncomfortable, huddled and peering into the late evening storm. Going aft to my cabin, I heard a flapping sound from under a winch and stopped to investigate. It was not a seabird, but a brown tawny owl caught out in the storm that had crash-landed aboard our ship seeking refuge from the storm. Winch beds were a collection point for excess grease and oil and seldom cleaned; this was left to Mother Nature in heavy seas. I took the owl to the safety of my cabin and spent the next few hours cleaning its matted feathers, tongue and beak with warm soapy water. I tried to feed it with morsels of raw meat, but it just stared at me, motionless. It lay helpless in the palm of my hand as I spoke soothing and encouraging words into the beautiful, unblinking hazel eyes that seemed to accept its fate without fuss. Finally, it gave a faint sigh, closed its eyes and went limp. Blowing air into its oily beak was to no avail. I went to my bunk with a heavy heart.

The next morning, I discreetly dropped the bird overboard and have never forgotten those beautiful eyes.

Eventually, we loaded cargo in the oppressive heat of the Persian Gulf, all aboard were pleased to be heading south, down the coast again with a cargo of crude oil for Europe. With the Suez Canal closed it was to be a long, boring thirty-six-day voyage around the African continent back to Europe. Once again in the Madagascar Channel we ran into another storm and I thought about the beautiful tawny owl.

Fully laden and low in the water we punched through the sea with mountains of green water constantly pounding across our decks. This time a huge albatross crash-landed aboard in broad daylight.

Every sailor knows that albatrosses are the ghosts of deceased mariners and that bad luck would befall any vessel on which an albatross died. There was great concern and eagerness to get the monster airborne as soon as possible. I was the volunteer.

With a borrowed oilskin jacket and dodging crashing waves, I crept toward the gigantic bird lodged behind a set of mooring bollards. The beak was the size of a pair of garden shears, the beady black eyes were full of malice, and the screeching was an angry warning to me.

I wrapped it up with a well-timed lunge of the oilskin as its clacking beak struck out at my head. It felt the size of an adult and with my adrenalin running high I threw both the snapping bird and the oilskin jacket overboard in an instant. They hit the nearest wave with a splash. We watched relieved, as the big bird shook off the oilskin, paddled away then soared back into the storm.

Again I remembered the beautiful tawny owl.

The Swiss Trip

Being a seaman, I thought a trip to Switzerland would have to be unique and exciting, although many well-travelled people warned me I would find it boring.

On leave again with another voyage over, I had received a letter from a fun-loving New Zealand girl I had met on my previous leave while touring Southern Ireland in a mobile home.

Susan was a cuddly, positively energetic twenty-two year-old on her first overseas experience. I was experienced and senior.

I had visited my ageing mother in Buckinghamshire for a week and it was time to put into practice the ideas I'd had in the endless idleness the voyage offered – to visit somewhere new each shore leave.

Life on tankers was often dull, with long periods at sea and very short times in ports that were often miles from the nearest towns. In the Persian Gulf there were no towns, no shore leave, just wired compounds with armed guards, gasping heat and a barren landscape of rocks and sand dominated by huge refineries and miles of oil pipes.

The cheerful letter from Susan was from Geneva. She had acquired an extension to her work permit and would love to see me again. My impulsive nature had me telephoning Swissair reservations at their London head office at 4.30pm on a Friday evening.

"I want to book a flight to Geneva, please."

"Certainly sir, when would you like to go?"

"Tomorrow, if possible."

"We have a flight departing Heathrow at 1300 hours and seats are available on that flight sir."

"OK, book me on that one please."

"Can you pay here before 6pm sir? We're closed tomorrow."

"Unfortunately not, but I'll pay cash at the airport desk on arrival."

"Can I have your name please, sir?"

"Yes, it's John Smith. No, no middle names."

The seventies were a time of constant terrorism with regular hijackings of planes around the globe, and in true British fashion I hadn't given it a second thought. After all, I'd been flying to far-flung ports to join or leave ships. I was a seasoned traveller.

The next day, with only a black weekend bag as luggage, I paid for my ticket and went to the crowded cafeteria bar for a limp white sandwich and strong brown tea. There I met a larrikin deckhand from my last voyage. He was drunk and unshaven and had spent all his hard-earned wages from the voyage in only one week, so he was off to join another tanker in Rotterdam. I gave him a five-pound note just as he boarded his flight, remembering times I'd been in the same situation. (Seamen looked after seamen in those days.)

Ten minutes later my flight was called and I joined the shuffling queue heading for the departure gate and Switzerland. My passage was blocked by a very tall, impeccably dressed man in a navy blue suit with a snow-white shirt behind a striped military tie. Not a single strand of Brylcreemed hair was out of place.

"Mr Smith, can I have your passport?" The voice was snobbish, upper class and weak. He didn't say please. I took an instant dislike to him.

"What for?" I asked loudly, while other passengers filed past with impartial glances.

"Just give me your passport and keep your voice down."

It was an order. I realised he was a cop of some sort and complied. He took a slim black book from his inside pocket and long slender fingers expertly flicked through both books at once. Handing me back my passport, he turned and walked into a room leaving me standing there nonplussed.

I rejoined the thinning queue, unsettled.

A man with a brown suit, wispy beard and black-rimmed glasses took my passport and handed it to a short bull-like figure. This chap had bulging green eyes, cauliflower ears, and a greying crewcut on his melon-shaped head. Banana-like fingers exposed my photograph and the green marble eyes stared at me. He seemed ready for a rugby scrum as I met his glare.

"Why are you going to Geneva?"

"To see a friend."

His undersized tweed jacket seemed ready to pop its leather buttons as he sucked air through his battered nose.

"When were you last there?"

"I've never been there before." I was getting annoyed again. "What the hell's this all about?"

"Shut up or you'll be put into the interview room for a strip search."

Now I was feeling anxious. I hadn't liked the tall poncy one, but this gorilla was almost an animal. Wispy-beard guy vainly searched my bag.

"On your way, John Smith. We're watching you."

"Would you like me to go back home?" I said sarcastically.

"You heard. On your way." He scowled, and I went.

I was a reluctant traveller. All other passengers were suspect.

My passport was double-checked on arrival, and uniforms and guns were everywhere. On edge, I finally reached the arrivals hall.

With a loud screech, Susan was there! But hanging round her neck was a handsome young Irish lad, ten years my junior.

"This is Liam! We're going to get married next month and you're the first to know and be invited!"

Her kiss was dry and his waiter's hand was damp.

Three days later I returned to London unchecked.

They were right. I found Switzerland boring.

The 'Tail' of Durban

It was October 1970. The *SS British Ambassador* belonged to the British Petroleum company and was in a Durban dry-dock for engine repairs.

It was my first trip back to sea after more than two years of enforced landlubbing after I had nearly killed a drunken shipmate in a fight over a visiting lady in the port of Vancouver. It had been self-defence but my rage had been unstoppable.

I had been a boatswain with the Shaw Savill line for some years but then had been unceremoniously dumped. I found a job as an assistant manager in a south London supermarket – a far cry from the life I loved. I fought my two year ban with the help of the Seamans' Union and eventually I was allowed to return. This was to be the one and only chance of getting back to sea, demoted back to able seaman (Take it or leave it.) I took it, and here I was, a cargo ship man on a bloody oil tanker.

An older tanker of 15,000 tons, she was crewed by the bad boys of the merchant navy and had been plying oil between the Persian Gulf and the Republic of South Africa for many years, and never went back to the UK ports. Chances were I could be away from home for two years. Rumour was rife the oil was going from Durban by rail to Rhodesia, which was enduring trade sanctions plus the British naval blockading of their sea ports in Mozambique.

Two others were flown out with me, a steward and a cook. Both were obnoxious Irish drunks. The previous cook had been sedated and removed from the vessel in a straitjacket on arrival in port. The steward had disappeared at sea one night. Both had been very close friends indeed. Too close, according to the rabble crew, but most ship's cooks in those days were drunks or crazy – often both. A prerequisite for the job, it seemed.

Like all dry-docks, it was organised chaos, understood only be a few of those who worked there. Huge plates were missing from the hull, the ship's turbines were stripped and taken ashore. Even the propeller was missing. The local labour force teemed like ants from stem to stern, perfectly-chiselled Africans singing and chanting while they worked.

Lugging my well-worn suitcase aft along the flying bridge, I found my Spartan single cabin was being used as the boilermakers' storage. There were heavy hammers pounding in the bowels and bilges below. Rust and dust choked the air. The toilets were locked and sealed, the water disconnected. Emergency lights barely lit the cluttered alleyways. It was to be my new home, and I was expected to sleep in this purgatory for the next six nights.

I hauled the suitcase ashore again and booked into a very comfortable hotel far away from the dockside pandemonium.

The owner booked me in and insisted on my passport for the police check and safekeeping. He also suggested I join him at the bar after I'd refreshed.

Rashad, the white-coated Indian lad, ceased attacking his acne and took my case to a suite on the first floor. A ceiling fan whirled and the evening breeze wafted the net curtains at the open French doors. The traffic noise below was a pleasant sound compared to the bedlam of the ship. Rashad poured a glass of iced orange juice for me, ran the bath, thanked me politely, pocketed my tip, said goodnight and was gone. I felt human again.

Later, feeling much better, I headed for the bar. The owner peeled away from a small group, hand outstretched. Jacob Stien was in his fifties. A gold filling matched his gold-rimmed glasses and he wore an immaculate powder-blue safari suit. There was a gold Omega watch on the wrist that handed me the iced rum and Coke. He steered me to a corner table and clinked his tonic water against my rum. (Doctor's orders, he explained.) He looked quickly over his shoulder and lowered his voice.

"Is your name really John Smith?" The accent was strongly Dutch more than South African. Flippantly I asked if his was really Jacob Stien. He laughed loudly then looked around the room again and returned to the lowered tone.

"My family came from Amsterdam after the war. We are Jewish, you understand. I changed my name from a very long and hard-to-pronounce Dutch name – it was easier back then. Hey, we have the same initials."

I accepted his offered cheroot. He lit it with a gold lighter, watching me closely through the smoke.

"Look John, you've been to South Africa before so you know the score. We all have to obey the rules otherwise there would be chaos here. So what's your real name?" He noted my rising testiness and spoke out of the side of his mouth. "I must report all comings and goings to the police – it's the law. They will be here to check in the morning." He stood, shook my hand, then left the room.

I sat and observed the twenty people in the bar. I wondered if a policeman was amongst them. The waiter and barman were coloured, everyone else was white and male, except for one Asian gent who stood alone at the bar. I joined him there and ordered another rum and Coke.

Mr Toshi, a Japanese businessman, spoke perfect English, was relaxed and smiling, and delicately sipped a Castle lager. I introduced myself.

"My ear tells me you're not South African John, but from London."

I felt more at ease with him than with Jacob. He hailed from Osaka and was pleased to know that I had been there on my second trip to sea in 1956. As the apartheid system was strictly adhered to by one and all, I was intrigued by his presence in this whites-only bastion.

His explanation came with an almost feminine chuckle and he didn't lower his voice as Jacob had.

"South Africa is so eager to attract international investment and business that we Japanese are afforded honorary white status, while my Chinese colleagues must book into a coloureds' hotel in another part of town."

We chatted easily for an hour until a taxi took him to the airport and Johannesburg.

I slept soundly on the big double bed under the turning fan.

When I emerged from my morning shower there was a man in my room. Rashad was also there but looked uneasy. His dark eyes flicked feverishly towards the stranger, sending me a silent signal. While Rashad changed the sheets, the stranger sat in the corner armchair, crossed his legs, lit a cigarette and watched me dress. Rashad finished his task, gave a last eye signal and left.

The stranger, slim, medium height, in his late twenties with short dark curly hair, remained mute. I was annoyed. I had a sudden urge to grab the cheeky bastard by his scrawny neck and eject him, but I knew he was police.

Finally he spoke. I didn't like his guttural accent or his tone.

"How long are you staying, John Smith?"

The prick still hadn't introduced himself, plus he knew my full name and expected an answer.

"Why do you ask?" Being uncommunicative was one of my strong points and by now I'd decided to enjoy the stonewalling and lower the famous Aries cone of silence on him.

"Just curious."

The reply was so ridiculously inane I had to stifle a laugh.

I had planned a walk around town to see the sights, especially the famous Indian markets. My mother-in-law back in London was Durban-born and had hoped I'd send back a special brand of curry powder unavailable in Britain at that time. But this interloper had temporarily altered my plans.

I was determined to milk this situation to the end. I phoned room service and ordered coffee for one, turned the radio to a pop music station, went to the bathroom and sat smoking a cigarette, hoping to find an empty room when I came out. But he was still in the chair when I returned ten minutes later.

Rashad brought the tray and I gave him a knowing wink. He ignored the now uncomfortable plod and left with a beaming smile.

It was now afternoon and the berk was still squatting in the chair, nameless. I locked my suitcase, purposely pocketing the keys, and went down the polished stairs to order a beer in the empty bar. In the mirrored shelving I noticed my shadow come in and take a seat by the door.

It was time for the old seaman's trick.

I finished my beer and ordered another, while the shadow pretended to read a magazine. I loudly told the barman I was going to my room for the local map. Leaving my beer, an empty cigarette pack and book of matches clearly visible on the bar, I sauntered through the door without a glance at the inept sentinel. Once through the hotel door I broke into a brisk walk, turned right twice, then hopped into a taxi and was rapidly lost in the traffic on my way to the markets.

Durban was instantly familiar. I'd visited many times in the past on the Union Castle liners and tramp ships. Like Cape Town it was one of my favourite ports.

After the markets I went to Durban's famous beach and met a beautiful German girl who thought I was German too. The sun set as we sat there on the sand talking about our families miles away. She had lost her husband-to-be in an autobahn accident a month before and was taking time out. I told her about my new family in south London and my beautiful baby daughter. She was happy for me, I was sad for her. I left her hopeful for her future and her beaming smile still lives within me. An evening to remember.

I returned late to the hotel to find the worried-looking policeman in a huddle with Jacob in the foyer. He had the nerve to ask me where I had been.

"Out" I smugly replied.

Back in my room I found my suitcase unlocked and deliberately left open. I fell asleep with a grin.

The next afternoon another stranger sat in the bar.

A week later I was swapping stories on the poopdeck of the *SS British Ambassador* on my way to the Persian Gulf and another story.

130

Britannic

Changing Times

They say there is nothing as constant as change, and many changes were in the air as Shaw Savill Lines' latest cargo ship was launched on the Clyde in 1967.

The *Britannic* was a ship of the future and the start of the many changes to come. Ships with cranes instead of derricks were already commonplace as were a number of purpose-built "heavy lift" ships.

Our foremast looked like a huge inverted tuning fork with a heavy lift "Jumbo" derrick that could work two holds at the same time. There was also a new device called the "Thompson swinging derrick" another heavy lift labour-saving idea that looked like a gooseneck derrick, but performed like a crane. Viewed from the horizon our mast appeared to be covered by a gigantic web, such was the mass of wires and winches that was required to operate this new-fangled set-up.

Grease nipples; grease nipples; grease nipples. They were everywhere, thousands of them. There was a special manual provided to help locate each and every one. A recalcitrant junior rating caught swinging the lead (shirking) spent at least three whole days with the grumpy carpenter filling and pumping a grease gun.

Shipboard sages rolled their eyes ruefully around the mess-rooms of the British Merchant Fleet and gloomily predicted the end. There was talk of huge un-manned ocean-going barges roaming the seas controlled by satellites and towed in and out of major ports that were run by computers.

The neatly folded tarpaulin corners of a ship's hatch, wedged, battened and ready for sea were already a thing of the past. Rolling steel hatch covers were now well established. At first these monsters claimed and maimed many unwary fingers and were responsible for gory accidents and even death.

Large steel boxes called containers began to appear as regular deck cargo. This new, secure way of shipping was resented by all light-fingered stevedores and seamen the world over. The fragile and expensive and sought-after cargoes like export whisky and gin were now safely out of reach.

Our colonial cousins in Australia resisted these advances through their unions, claiming job losses. Many bitter strikes gave them a chance to enjoy more of the Christmas summer holidays and more time for the beach and BBQs.

One famous Australian Dockers strike was when "Embarrassment Money" was demanded for unloading toilet pans, even though they were created by the famous British Royal Doulton company and carried the Queen of England's seal of approval. From that moment on all future shipments of "Pommie Poo-Pots" were "containerised" and another problem was solved with the changing times.

Job protection was a strange argument in New Zealand. The biggest problem was a genuine shortage of a population to support a reasonable workforce to handle the demand for exports of all things dairy New Zealand. The wool from the sheep's back, the carcass, the liver, the kidneys, the hoofs and even the eyeballs were in high demand back in Britain and Europe. "Seagulls" were used to unload and reload the numerous ships that idled away many unproductive weeks in all the ports around New Zealand. "Seagulls" were locals who made themselves available for work aboard the ships in port. Off-duty bus and taxi drivers, policemen, students, farmers and general layabouts all mingled in organised chaos with the regular "wharfies" who were only known for their speed at "knockoff time". "Seagulling" was a very lucrative occupation in the "Slowzone" of New Zealand. The locals called it Godzone.

Some considered New Zealand to be at the bottom of the world and the port of Bluff to be its sphincter. When Bluff joined with the changing times by introducing an all-weather conveyer belt to load the refrigerated ships with frozen sheep carcasses around the clock, even the Luddites welcomed this piece of new technology. Any shortening of the time spent in Bluff was considered a blessing.

In each port the eager local press reported on this latest maritime marvel that could almost discharge its own cargo. "seagulls" were not required on the *Britannic* or her sister ship, the *Majestic*.

The chief mate was a hardworking Welshman who constantly referred to time as 'The Old Enemy'. It was rumoured that even when asleep he kept one eye on the clock. He was a good mate on a good ship and everything ran like clockwork.

During the voyage the oil tanker *Torrey Canyon* ran aground at Land's End on England's southern coast with 120,000 tons of crude oil aboard. A few days later it was bombed by the R.A.F and the released oil was then set alight with incendiary bombs. Good practice for the chaps and a chance to yell "tallyho" again.

The new Cunard liner *Queen Elizabeth 2* was launched on the Clyde and a week later the old *Queen Mary* arrived at Southampton from her final Atlantic crossing.

As the Vietnam war raged on, above our heads the space race was in full flight with the Russians landing probes on Venus while America's Mariner and Saturn rockets cruised the outer atmosphere. In Cape Town, South Africa, the first human heart transplant was a success.

There were plenty of yarns to spin on the *Britannic* poop deck homeward bound.

Finally, as I lowered my suitcase onto Valerie's front doorstep I heard a wailing song on her radio,

'The Times they are a Changing'.

Shipping today – container ships

The End

11713726R00080

Printed in Great Britain
by Amazon.co.uk, Ltd.,
Marston Gate.